D1277165

Our Debt to Greece and Rome

EDITORS

GEORGE DEPUE HADZSITS, PH.D.

DAVID MOORE ROBINSON, PH.D., LL.D.

SURVIVALS OF ROMAN RELIGION

BY

GORDON J. LAING

COOPER SQUARE PUBLISHERS, INC.
NEW YORK
1963

Published 1963 by Cooper Square Publishers, Inc.
59 Fourth Avenue, New York 3, N. Y.
Library of Congress Catalog Card No. 63-10280

TO

MAURICE HUTTON

PRINCIPAL EMERITUS OF
UNIVERSITY COLLEGE IN
THE UNIVERSITY OF TORONTO
FOR FIFTY YEARS THE MAINSTAY
OF CLASSICAL STUDIES
IN CANADA

"When one religion finally supplants another, it generally takes over from its predecessor such of. its usages as seem harmless or praiseworthy."

LEGGE, *Forerunners and Rivals of Christianity*, 1.84–85.

PREFACE

IN THIS treatment of survivals the term
"Roman religion" has been used with its
current comprehensiveness and so includes
all the cults, of whatever provenance, that
found a following in Rome. It is not of course
a logical designation but it has the merit of being a convenient one. Strictly speaking, "Roman religion" would mean that animism which
prevailed before the period of the Tarquin
dynasty when Greek influence, streaming into
Rome from Etruria on the north and Magna
Graecia on the south, transformed the whole
system through the introduction of imitative
temples and borrowed statue types. Nor did
the process of transformation and accretion
cease with the introduction of gods and forms
of ritual from other parts of Italy and from
Greece. As early as the Hannibalic war the
Romans showed interest in the worship of Cy-

bele, the Great Mother of the Gods, a Phrygian nature-goddess, and established her cult on the Palatine Hill. Later other Oriental divinities were introduced, and although many of them failed to obtain recognition by the state they formed an important part of the religious complex in Rome and Italy. Still another element in the situation was the cult of the deified emperors which, initiated by the deification of Julius Caesar, flourished till the time of Maxentius.

Of the nature of these religions and of the history of their development in Rome no attempt has been made to give a detailed or systematic account in this essay. Only those cults or phases of cults have been mentioned of which there seem to be survivals, and in the case of those mentioned only enough has been said to clarify the background of the survival. It is only with survivals, that is with the " debt " of later civilization to the religious beliefs and practices of the Romans, that the book is concerned.

The order of presentation is only roughly chronological. The survivals of indigenou cults are given first, and these are followed by a discussion of the traces that remain of the foreign gods worshipped in Rome and of emperor-worship. Then various relics of ancient religious belief, ritual or practice have been described, and at the end a brief account of material remains has been added.

The precarious character of any study in survivals — for the subject is even more perilous than the search for traces of influence in literary genetics — has been kept in mind throughout, and the plan has been to designate nothing as a survival till after careful scrutiny. The intemperate tone of some of the writings on the subject — for example Trede's books which, though containing much valuable information, are marred by exaggeration and hostility to the Church — has been sufficient warning of the danger of hasty conclusions. And in cases where it has been difficult to distinguish between survivals and parallels — and these are numerous — the available data, often obviously inadequate, have been given and the decision left to the reader.

Baffling as the study of survivals often is, it is none the less interesting, and the number and importance of the remains become more and more impressive as one pursues the quest. For the investigation of the subject, by showing that so many old beliefs and forms of ritual, instead of perishing, have been drawn into the fabric of modern religion, brings home more vividly than any other kind of inquiry the conviction of the continuity of religious experience.

CONTENTS

[xi]

CONTENTS

SURVIVALS OF ROMAN
RELIGION

SURVIVALS OF ROMAN RELIGION

I. THE DEPARTMENTAL IDEA OF DEITY AND ITS SURVIVAL IN THE VENERATION OF SAINTS

1. THE OLD ROMAN PANDEMONISM

THE EARLIEST Roman religion of which we have any record was a system of pandemonism. There was a spirit — a demon it was often called — in every object, every act, every process and sometimes in every stage of a process. There is no better example of this than the succession of spirits that watched over each period of a man's life from birth to death. Juno Lucina, Candelifera and the Carmentes aided at birth. It was Vagitanus only who could inspire the first cry. Cunina guarded the infant in its cradle, giving place to Cuba when the small Roman attained the distinction of a bed. By

Rumina he was taught how to take his mother's milk; Edusa and Potina watched over him in the days of his weaning. Fabulinus taught him to talk; Statilinus to stand; Abeona and Adeona attended him in his first ventures from the house; as he grew to maturity Catius sharpened his wits, Sentia deepened his feeling, while Volumna stiffened his will. And so he was passed from god to god and the long line of divine relays only ended when Viduus parted body and soul. Extreme specialization is also seen in the list of twelve spirits to whom the priest of Ceres appealed at the beginning of the sowing season. The special functions of these covered every stage in the growing of crops from the breaking of the soil to the storing and distribution of the grain. The names of these spirits are, like those of the spirits of the periods of life just mentioned, obviously derived from their special activities: [1] e.g., Obarator (*arare,* to plough), Sarritor (*sarrire,* to hoe), Messor (*metere,* to reap), and Conditor (*condere,* to store). Another instance of this characteristic of Roman religion is seen in the case of the

---

[1] The full list is: Vervactor, Reparator, Imporcitor, Insitor, Obarator, Occator, Sarritor, Subruncinator, Messor, Convector, Conditor and Promitor.

house, every part of which had its guardian divinity, as Servius points out in his commentary on Virgil,[2] where he specifies Forculus (*fores,* door), Cardea (*cardo,* hinge), and Limentinus (*limen,* threshold).

But the evidence of this particularistic character of Roman religion is not confined to these lists of obscure spirits. The gods of the Roman pantheon in general — even the greatest of them — showed, in their origin at least, a high degree of specialization. In some cases the original function of the divinity expanded in different directions but in others the early specialization maintained its old limits. Janus was the god of the door, Vesta of the hearth, Faunus of the forest, Pales of pasture land, Fons of springs, Volturnus of running streams, Saturn of sowing, Ceres of growth, Flora of blossom, Pomona of fruit, and Consus of harvest. Even the great god Jupiter, manifold as his powers subsequently became, was at first only the spirit of the bright sky.[3]

It is not necessary to give other examples of

---

[2] *Aeneid,* II. 469: singula (membra) enim domus sacrata sunt deis.

[3] See Rose's discussion of Roman polydemonism in *Primitive Culture in Italy,* 44.

this tendency. It pervaded the whole religious system. Its persistence, either with or without modification, in the case of the well-known gods of Rome is too familiar a fact to require comment. And there can be but little doubt that the highly specialized demonism exemplified by the lists given at the beginning of this chapter endured also to some extent in the later periods. Doubtless the introduction of gods from foreign countries and the development of an elaborate ritual in some of the Greek or Oriental cults diverted the minds of many from the old system. But there is no evidence that it ever completely passed away, and there must have been many people, especially in the rural districts, whose belief in a world swarming with spirits differed but little from that of their remote progenitors. Particularization was too inherent a part of Roman religious belief to yield entirely to any influence. Plutarch speaks of spirits who carried men's wishes to the higher gods. Maximus of Tyre tells us of minor deities who healed disease, aided men in various crises, accompanied and watched over them, and guarded cities and countryside. The stories of miraculous cures in temples told in his *Sermones sacri* by the rhetorician Aristides who lived in the time of Marcus Aurelius attest the widespread belief in manifold agencies of super-natural assistance.[4] The vogue of the Neo-platonic philosophy in the third century after Christ resulted in a renewal of belief in the existence of great numbers of subordinate and intermediate spirits. Nor has there ever been a satisfactory demonstration of the theory that in enumerating the names of these minute and obscure departmental deities the Church Fathers were merely resurrecting from earlier records, for purposes of ridicule, religious conceptions that had long ceased to be current.

So much for the pandemonism of the ancient Romans. Enough has been said to show how deeply rooted in their minds this attitude toward supernatural powers was. It was one of the most important phases of their religious consciousness and was to such an extent of the very essence of their faith that it was bound to survive. And survive it did. For though there is a notable difference in the character of the supernatural beings that in the fourth century succeeded to the multitudinous functions of the

[4] Trede, *Das Heidenthum in der römischen Kirche,* *Anhang,* I. 317.

old departmental spirits, there is little or no change in the attitude of mind. Such a document as the *Sermones sacri* of Aristides mentioned above demonstrates the facility of the transition from the old to the new, from the pagan to the Christian. For Aristides' accounts of wonderful cures have often been spoken of as forerunners of the legends of Saints.

2. THE VENERATION OF SAINTS

AND it is in the doctrine of the veneration of Saints that the polytheism of the old departmental deities survives. It may be that the founders of Christianity found that the belief of the people — especially the illiterate class — in these specialized spirits of minor grade was one of their greatest problems. They recognized the people's predilection for spirits that would help in specific situations, and they realized also that the masses felt more at home with beings who, while of divine nature or associations, were not too far removed from the human level. They were keenly interested in winning the pagans to the faith and they succeeded. But undoubtedly one element in their success was the inclusion in their system of the doctrine of the veneration of Saints. They seem to

have felt that in order to make any headway
at all, it was necessary for them to match the
swarms of spirits available for the pagans with
a multitude of wonder-working saints and martyrs. How far they were prepared to go is indicated by their favorable attitude toward the
pagan veneration of Virgil that amounted almost to deification. Apparently most of the
churchmen of the period of the conflict of religions proclaimed the greatness of Virgil and
placed him almost on a level with the biblical
prophets. They sought evidence of the truth of
Christianity in pagan literature and insisted
that Virgil had prophesied the coming of
Christ. Everyone is familiar with the mass
of literature that has grown up around the so-
called Messianic Eclogue. Not only Virgil was
glorified but also the pagan Sibyls who were
thought to have inspired his words. The Sibyls
too were given a place beside the Old Testament prophets.

There have been many discussions of the
relation of the doctrine of the veneration of
Saints to various phases of Roman religion,
ranging from the notably temperate treatment
of Lucius [5] to the more positive statements

[5] *Die Anfänge des Heiligenkults.*

[9]

of Renan [6] and Harnack [7] and the uncompromising assertions of Trede,[8] " P. Saintyves " [9] and Salomon Reinach.[10] Renan for example says that any peasant who prays to a particular saint for a cure for his horse or ox or drops a coin into the box of a miraculous chapel is in that act pagan. He is responding to the prompting of a religious feeling that is older than Christianity and so deep-set that Christianity has not been able to root it out. Harnack sees in the veneration of Saints nothing but a recrudescence of pagan polytheism.

The term " veneration of Saints " has been used advisedly. For in any fair discussion of this subject it should be remembered that the Church has never taught the worship of Saints. Every enlightened churchman knows this, but whether the peasants of southern Italy and other parts of Europe distinguish with any degree of precision between veneration and worship is another question. It is not likely that they do, and for those who are looking for evidence of the continuance of the creative

[6] *Hibbert Lectures,* 32.
[7] *Lehrbuch der Dogmengeschichte,* II. 442.
[8] *Op. cit., passim.*
[9] *Les Saints, successeurs des dieux.*
[10] *Orpheus. Histoire générale des religions.*

power of Roman religion, the beliefs of the illiterate are of as much importance as the formulated doctrines of the Church. Our subject is not survivals of paganism in the modern Church but survivals in modern times.

A good example of the closeness of the resemblance of the specialization of function of different Saints to that of pagan spirits is found in the published lists of Saints used by Spanish peasants. The very publication of the list emphasizes the similarity of the situation to that which existed in ancient Roman times, when the people, overwhelmed by the number and multiplicity of names of the departmental deities, used to appeal to the official list kept by the pontiffs. Here are some of the examples furnished by the Spanish index: San Serapio should be appealed to in case of stomache-ache; Santa Polonia for toothache; San José, San Juan Bautista and Santa Catalina for headache; San Bernardo and San Cirilo for indigestion; San Luis for cholera; San Francisco for colic; San Ignacio and Santa Lutgarda for childbirth; Santa Balsania for scrofula; San Felix for ulcers; Santa Agueda for nursing mothers; San Babilas for burns; San Gorge for an infected cut; Santa Quiteria for dog's bite;

San Ciriaco for diseases of the ear; Santa Lucia for the eyes; Santa Bibiana for epilepsy; San Gregorio for frost-bite; San Pantaleon for haemorrhoids; San Roque for the plague; Santa Dorothea for rheumatism; San Pedro for fever; and Santa Rita for the impossible!

There is a similar list for southern Italy, the Saints and their functions sometimes coinciding with the Spanish classification but in other cases showing variations. San Roque for example is associated with cases of plague in Italian legends [11] just as in Spain. To the Italians also the intercession of Santa Lucia is efficacious for sore eyes. San Giuseppe, however, to south Italians seems to be connected with the interpretation of dreams. Giuseppe had interpreted dreams to Pharaoh during his life time, and it was believed that he retained his interest in them after death. [12] Santa Anna

[11] Jameson, *Sacred and Legendary Art*, II. 425 ff.
[12] Among other things San Giuseppe is sometimes asked to bring his suppliant luck in the next drawing of the lottery:

> O casto Giuseppe
> Che spiegaste i sogni
> A Faraone
> Portatemi tre numeri
> Per questa estrazione.

is the patron Saint of women in childbirth in Naples and its neighborhood. The prayers addressed to her are strikingly like those with which pagan women appealed to Juno Lucina; and perhaps it is not entirely fanciful to trace a connection between the candles with which Santa Anna is worshipped and Lucina (from *lux*, light), the epithet of Juno as a goddess of childbirth.

The similarity in attitude of mind of pagan and Christian devotees and the survival of the polytheistic idea in modern times may be seen in a comparison of the behavior of the people who watched the procession which preceded the circus games in ancient Rome and that of the crowd which fills the streets of Naples today on the occasion of the festival held in May in honor of San Gennaro, the patron saint of the city. In the old Roman procession a conspicuous place was given to the images of the gods that were borne along in floats; and as they were carried past, pious Romans called upon the names of those whom they regarded as their special protectors. So too at the Naples festival. In the procession referred to the images of many Saints, each of them with his own place in the affections of the Neapolitan proletariat, are carried from the Cathedral to the Church of Santa Chiara. Saints of all centuries are there, some of whom attained the dignity hundreds of years ago, while others are more recent creations. As the procession moves along, persons in the crowd call out the name of their patron Saint, and when the image of San Biagio — a sort of Christian Aesculapius with special powers in diseases of the throat — passes by, the Neapolitan mothers hold up their croupy bambini and implore a remedy.

But it is not only in southern Europe that the ancient particularism of divine function still survives. For example in Prussia St. Goar is the patron of potters, St. Crispin of shoemakers; St. Nicholas of boatmen; St. Apollonia cures tooth-ache; St. Laurence rheumatism; and St. Agatha is guardian of the household fire.[13] In the region of the Vosges St. Catharine helps women find husbands, St. Sabina cures the pangs of love, while St. Abdon is believed to drive away fleas.[14] This special-

[13] Kerler, *Die Patronate der Heiligen;* Deubner, *De incubatione.*

[14] Kroll, in article on " Momentary Gods," in Hastings, *Encyclopedia of Religion and Ethics* (referred to in this book as *E. R. E.*), VIII. 778.

ization of the Saints is clearly recognized in the *Diario Romano* where St. Blaise, St. Liberius and St. Martha are assigned curative powers in the case of sore throat, gallstone, and epidemics respectively.

II. GODS OF THE FAMILY

1. THE LARES

CHIEF among the domestic gods were the Lares, called Lares domestici or Lares familiares indifferently, who together with the Penates were regularly worshipped in the Roman household. Originally there had been only one Lar familiaris,[1] but from about the beginning of the first century B.C. they were two in number, and as we know from the statuettes and the paintings found at Pompeii and elsewhere, they were commonly represented in the form of youthful dancing figures. In houses of the humbler type these little images were generally kept in a niche near the hearth in the *atrium* (which was often kitchen, dining room, and living room in one), but in the more pretentious dwellings they were placed in a small shrine (*lararium*), a sort of miniature temple on a pedestal which stood in a corner of the *atrium* or peristyle. They were

[1] Cf. the prologue of Plautus' *Aulularia*.

[16]

the guardian spirits of the family and watched over its safety and prosperity. Their worship was part of the daily life of the Romans. An offering of food and wine was made to them by the master of the house after the chief course of the dinner every day. And there were special offerings to them on occasions of particular importance, such as a birth, a naming or a wedding. Many fond references to these "little gods" are made by the poets. Horace [2] for example tells of their images crowned with rosemary and myrtle, and Tibullus [3] recalls the days of his childhood when he played about their feet. One cannot read such passages as these without realizing that the attitude of the Romans toward them was one of affection, and that in the whole pantheon there were no gods nearer or dearer to them than these. All the members of the family seem to have felt the closeness of the relation; it was a part of their religious heritage. For while they knew of other and more powerful divinities, they had not been brought up in such intimate contact with any of them and so never attained the degree of familiarity and homely constancy of

[2] *Od.*, III. 23. 15.
[3] I. 10. 15.

faith that they felt toward the Lares. In this distinctive quality of the Romans' attitude toward them lies the explanation of the fact that their worship more than any other resisted the influence of the Greek and Oriental cults imported into Rome. It showed little or no change through the regal, republican and imperial periods.

For this study, however, the significant fact is not that the cult lasted through the whole period of the Empire but that it has not even yet entirely disappeared. The belief in these friendly and protecting house-spirits was so closely woven into the religious consciousness of the people that in various parts of Italy it survived the passing of that religious system of which it had originally been a part. For example the house-spirit — called Monacello, " Little Monk " — whose diminutive wooden image is found in so many peasants' houses in the neighborhood of Naples and Salerno, is a survival of the Roman Lar; [4] and the same is true of the Aguriellu, " Little Augur," the spirit of the household that is seen so often in the houses of the peasantry in Calabria.[5]

[4] Trede, *op. cit.*, I. 127.
[5] Dorsa, *La Tradizione greco-latina*, 115.

These are specific survivals of the cult of the Lar.

In another example, of far greater interest on account of its implications, we find not direct survival indeed but a very strong probability of influence. This is the case of the figurines of the infant Jesus found in houses on the island of Capri.[6] These are made of wood, just as the Roman Lares often were, and in size and equipment resemble their ancient prototypes. But images of this class are not confined to Capri. The most famous of all these figurines of the child Christ is the Santissimo Bambino of the Church of S. Maria in Aracoeli on the Capitoline Hill in Rome. This image has had a long and interesting history. It is believed that when loaned to some faithful member of the Church and taken to his house it bestows blessings on his family. Placed on the bed of some invalid it is thought to bring relief from suffering and restoration to health. In a word it has been a source of comfort, encouragement, and well-being to afflicted families just as the Lares were in the days of old.

A legend of the Penates, domestic spirits closely associated with the Lares, is matched by

[6] Trede, *op. cit.*, II. 210.

a story told of this image of the Bambino. It is said that on one occasion when it had been stolen, it found its way back to the Church. This, it will be noticed, is substantially the same story as that told about the oldest Penates in the history of Rome. For when Aeneas' son Ascanius, after his father's death, took the Penates from Lavinium to Alba Longa, they returned of their own accord to Lavinium, and it was then decided to leave them there.[7] While this tale, which is obviously an aetiological legend invented to explain the continuance of the worship of the Roman Penates at Lavinium, may have been transferred directly from them to the Bambino, it is more likely that the story about the latter arose independently, similarity in conception of deity resulting in similarity of legend.

In other places in Italy it is the Madonna that has succeeded the Lar as the spirit of the household; in still others Saints are found with a similar function.[8]

So far only one class of Lares has been mentioned, namely Lares domestici or familiares. But there were many other kinds. In fact, as I

[7] Preller-Jordan, *op. cit.*, II. 162.
[8] Daremberg-Saglio, *Dictionnaire*, III[2]. 947.

have pointed out elsewhere,[9] it is probable that the word Lares is a generic term for spirits, and their special field is indicated in each case by the epithet. Of some of these other classes of Lares we find survivals in the veneration of Saints in modern times. For example, the old tradition that it was the Lares publici, also called the Lares praestites, the guardian spirits of the whole community, who drove Hannibal away when he appeared before the walls of Rome in 211 B.C., has its analogue in the story that St. Matthew, who is the patron Saint of Salerno and whose bones are said to lie in the crypt of the Cathedral there, on more than one occasion drove away the pirate fleets of the Saracens and saved the city. Another well-known class of Lares was that of the Lares compitales, the spirits of the crossroads. There were innumerable shrines in their honor throughout the rural districts. Moreover, especially from the time of Augustus, many sanctuaries had been erected to them at street corners in Rome and other cities. Of the popularity of this worship of crossroads spirits there is adequate evidence, and of its survival substantial indications are found in the attacks

[9] *Classical Philology*, XVI, 124–40 (1921).

made by mediaeval writers on the custom of
offering sacrifices and lighting candles at crossroads.[10] Nor can it be doubted that the common practice in Italy and other countries of
erecting chapels to saints at crossroads goes
back ultimately to the pagan worship of
the Lares compitales. Apparently the earlier
churchmen found that it was impossible to
divert the people from their crossroads superstitions, and so they adopted a plan that they
used on many other occasions. They tacitly
recognized the sanctity of the site, but by sub-
stituting Christian saints for pagan spirits they
succeeded in giving the religious aspirations of
the devotees a new direction. Of the strength
of the belief in the efficacy of these wayside
shrines, we have evidence in an incident of the
epidemic of cholera in Naples in 1884. The
people attributed the scourge to the walling up
of many of the niches that had been used as
street shrines. So vehement was their protest
that the old niches were reopened and many
new ones added. The effect on the Neapoli-
tans was precisely the same as that recorded so
often for the Romans by Livy and other ancient
writers, when proper measures had been taken

[10] Cf. Caspari, *Kirchenhist. Anecdota,* I. 172, 175.

to placate divinities to the neglect of whose rites they attributed the affliction of a plague or some other disaster.

2. THE GENIUS

THE pagan idea of tutelary spirits dominating particular fields contributed also to the Christian conception of angels. It was not the chief source of the belief, which goes back to Jewish or Chaldaean traditions, but it influenced certain phases of the doctrine. Mention has already been made of the numerous spirits which watched over the different stages of life. In addition to these there was a guardian spirit for every man and woman — a sort of double or *alter ego* who attended one through life. The spirit for men was called Genius, that for women Juno. It was so closely bound up with the person that it was not infrequently identified with him. "To indulge one's Genius" in Latin means to indulge one's self; "to take care of one's Genius" is the equivalent of taking care of one's self.

This idea had influence on the early Christian conception of angels. The fathers of the Church taught that every one had his guardian angel who attended him from the day of his birth to his death. Touching descriptions of the devotion of angels to their charges are found in Christian literature; and students of Dante will recall that passage where the guardian angel visits the sinner in purgatory, comforts him with the thought that his expiation will end at last, and finally when the term of suffering is over bears him to the Savior.[11]

Although the Church has never given formal recognition to the belief, Christianity has none the less its guardian angels. Chief among them is the archangel Raphael, guardian spirit of all humanity, whóse function as inherited from Hebrew sources found ready acceptance among the early Christians in Italy in whose religious beliefs tutelary spirits held so important a place.[12] But there are other guardian angels also. Certainly from Silvio Pellico's *Le Mie Prigioni* one gets the impression of an Italian belief not in one guardian spirit only but in many. And in Naples there is an annual festival of the Angeli Custodi.

[11] *Purgatorio,* C. VIII.
[12] The famous painter Raffaello, who was the son of Giovanni Santi of Urbino, was so named because he was born on the festival day of this guardian angel.

III. SERPENT–WORSHIP

IN POMPEIAN houses and elsewhere we frequently find a serpent or a pair of serpents associated with the Lares and the Genius of the paterfamilias — the "three gods" mentioned in one of the Pompeian wall-inscriptions.[1] Some paintings represent the serpent as coiled around an altar; others as approaching the altar to partake of the offerings that had been laid upon it; while still others show two serpents, male and female, crawling toward the altar from either side. So far as we can determine, these serpents are connected with the Genius. The subject, however, is an obscure one, and even the ancients were sometimes in doubt about it. When Virgil speaks of the serpent that crept from Anchises' tomb, he represents Aeneas as uncertain whether it was the Genius of the place or an attendant of his father.[2] At any rate, whatever the significance of the serpents

---

[1] *C. I. L.* IV. 1679: habeas propiteos deos tuos tres!
[2] *Aeneid,* V. 95: Geniumne loci famulumne parentis esse putet.

may have been, the painted representations of
them were common in Roman dwellings, and
we know from many sources that tame snakes
were often kept in houses.[3]

This serpent-cult has not entirely passed
away. In southern Italy, especially in Calabria, harmless snakes are kept as house-pets.[4]
They are regarded moreover as the incarnation
of protecting spirits and the departure of one
of them from its home portends disaster for
the household.

The Romans associated serpents with other
deities besides the Genius. Snakes were kept
in the precinct of the temple of Aesculapius on
the island in the Tiber, and there were some
also in one of the temple-buildings of the Bona
Dea on the Aventine. But the cult of Aesculapius was a Greek importation, and that of the
Bona Dea, although originally Roman, was
under strong Greek influence.[5] The serpent-

[3] Pliny, *N. H.*, XXIX. 4. 22. 72; Servius on *Aeneid*, V.
95; Fowler, *Roman Festivals* (referred to in this book as
R. F.), 104.

[4] Dorsa, *op. cit.*, 28. He says that even lizards are so
treated.

[5] Bona Dea was not at first the name of the divinity.
It was merely a descriptive term applied to the old in-
digenous deity Fauna. On the identification of the Bona
Dea Fauna with the Greek goddess Damia, whose cult

worship in the cult of Aesculapius therefore was certainly Greek and in that of Bona Dea probably so. But there is no evidence of foreign influence in the case of the serpent connected with the cult of Juno Sospita of Lanuvium. It was kept in a cave near the sanctuary and the story of its use as a test of virginity is told by Propertius [6] and other writers.

What has been said shows that serpents had a place in more than one kind of Roman religious observance: namely in the worship of the household gods, in that of divinities of healing (for the Bona Dea was active in this field as well as Aesculapius), and in such a cult as that of Juno Sospita who was primarily connected with the functions of women. It is indeed probable that serpent-worship was indigenous in Italy at an early period. The ready acceptance by the Romans of the serpents associated with Aesculapius or any other Greek divinity was in all likelihood due to the fact that no new or strange idea of divinity was

probably came to Rome from Tarentum, the Roman features of the worship fell into desuetude. Cf. Wissowa. *Religion und Kultus der Römer* (referred to in this book as *R. u. K.*), 216.

[6] IV. 8.

involved. The conception was one with which the natives of Italy had been familiar from time immemorial. And we may reasonably trace back to ancient times the widespread belief in southern Italy that a snakeskin is a magical agency. It is put under the pillow of the sick. Moreover, it is probable that we have a survival of an ancient cult in that annual procession at Cocullo (near the country of the ancient Marsi) in which men bearing live serpents pass before the statue of S. Domenico of Foligno, itself also hung with serpents. And we find an odd example of the endurance of local beliefs in the fact that the people of this region today regard themselves as immune from snake-bite and endowed with special power in the taming of serpents. For, as we know from ancient sources,[7] the Marsi of old prided themselves on similar qualifications.

[7] Pliny, *N. H.*, XXI. 13. 45. 78; XXVIII. 3. 6. 30; Gellius, XVI. 11; Solinus, 2. 27. Cf. *E. R. E.*, XI. 404.

IV. GODS OF MARRIAGE

WHILE civil marriage was an old institution among the Romans, the most ancient marriage rite of the patricians (*confarreatio*) involved the participation of religious functionaries. Sacrifice and prayer were part of the ceremony, and there was a procession to the bridegroom's house in the course of which appeals were made to the gods of marriage. Even after the confarreate marriage rite had become obsolete many of its characteristics survived in the form of wedding most frequently practiced by the Romans of the republican and imperial periods.

There was a ceremony of betrothal, which sometimes took place long before the wedding. On this occasion the prospective bridegroom gave his fiancée a ring which she wore on the third finger of her left hand. Sometimes guests were invited, and the bride-to-be received presents.

Great care was taken in the choice of the day

for the wedding. Certain seasons, on account of the nature of the religious rites that fell within them, were regarded as distinctly inauspicious, namely the month of May,[1] the first half of June,[2] the third week in February,[3] the first half of March, and some other single days, including all Kalends, Nones, and Ides. Moreover festival days in general were avoided.

The bride wore a veil over her head and was crowned with a wreath of flowers. In the later period it was usual for the bridegroom also to wear a garland. The ceremony included prayer, sacrifice, and the clasping of the right hands of bride and groom. In the rite of *confarreatio* the bride formally renounced her own family name and took that of her husband, and they both partook of the sacred cake, *libum farreum,* so named because it was made of the coarse wheat called *far.*

After the ceremony and the wedding feast, both of which generally took place in the bride's

[1] The festival of the Lemuria, connected with the cult of the dead, was held in this month; as also the rite of the Argei.

[2] The period of ancient rites at the temple of Vesta.

[3] The time of the Parentalia, when rites were celebrated at the tombs of deceased members of the family.

father's house, there was a procession to the new home, in which not only the bridal party but the general public took part. On reaching her husband's house the bride smeared the door-posts with fat or oil and bound them with woolen fillets. She was then lifted over the threshold and taken into the *atrium* of the house, where she prayed for a happy married life and made her first offering to the gods of the household.

Among the forms of marriage practiced by the Romans one was called *usus*. The consent of the contracting parties constituted the marriage, but it was only after a wife had lived with her husband for a year without absenting herself from his house for three successive nights that she passed, so far as her property was concerned, from her father's to her husband's control.

The Church maintained the pagan contact of marriage with religion, and though in the process of adaptation the content of the service was materially changed, many of the old customs were retained. Among the survivals may be mentioned the engagement-ring, still worn on the third finger of the left hand, the choice of the wedding-day, the bridal veil, the wedding feast and in some countries the wearing of garlands by both bride and groom, the procession to the bridegroom's house and the carrying of the bride over the threshold.

In regard to the giving of a ring it seems probable, in spite of Tertullian's [4] comment on the pagan character of the custom, that it was usual among most of the Christians even in his time (about A.D. 200), and it is quite clear that it was a universal practice from the fourth century.

In the matter of the prohibition of certain seasons for weddings a feeling similar to that which actuated the Romans may be found in modern times in the avoidance of Twelfth Night, Walpurgis Night (when witches are abroad), and the month of May.

While the ultimate origin of the veiling of the bride is uncertain, it is probably of religious significance. Perhaps the belief was that on so important and critical an event as marriage every precaution must be taken to ward off evil influences. Whatever its origin, it has come down to us not only in connection with weddings but also in the ceremony of "taking the veil" by Christian nuns. Their

[4] *De Idol.*, 16.

dedication to a life of devotion is regarded as a mystical marriage with Christ.[5]

Tertullian denounced the wearing of garlands by bride and groom as a heathen practice, but none the less they were worn both in his day and afterwards.[6] The custom still obtains in parts of Germany and Switzerland, and has never been abandoned in the countries whose religion is under the control of the eastern Church. It is possible, however, that in this matter the early Christians may have been influenced by Jewish as well as by Roman precedent. Jewish practice may also have been contributory to the continuance of the wedding feast. Wedding-processions that reproduce many of the features of those of pagan times — including the unrestrained raillery and uncensored jokes — may be seen in some parts of Italy today.[7]

The custom of carrying the bride across the threshold has continued in parts of England and Scotland.[8] The more or less plausible suggestion that this is a survival of the primi-

[5] Duchesne, *Christian Worship*, 422.
[6] Sidonius Apollinaris, Carmen 2, *Ad Anthem*.
[7] McDaniel, *Roman Private Life and Its Survivals*, 50.
[8] Gregor, *Folklore of North East of Scotland*, 51; Trumbull, *Threshold Covenant*, 26.

tive institution of " marriage by capture " has often been made, and this may be the right explanation. On the whole, however, it is likely that the act is part of a ritual intended to safeguard the reception and establishment of a stranger in the house. For the bride was a stranger to her husband's family and so in primitive psychology involved possibilities of peril to it.

Of the Roman marriage by *usus* it has been suggested that the custom of *hand-festing,* attested for a Dumfries county fair in the eighteenth century, was a survival.[9] At that fair it was customary for unmarried men or women to choose a companion for the year. At the end of that period, if they so decided, the marriage became permanent. If they preferred to separate, they could do so. In later times when this region fell under the control of the Abbot of Melrose, a priest was sometimes called in to confirm the marriage. Now this place was close to the old Roman camp at Castleoe'r, and it has been suggested that the *hand-festing* may have had its origin in the Roman *usus,* the participation of the priest being a Christian accretion. This is interesting but hardly

[9] Brand, *Popular Antiquities,* II. 88.

probable. It is a parallel to, rather than a survival of, the Roman custom. There are traces of *hand-festing* in other parts of England and Scotland and it was common among the ancient Danes.

V. GODS OF FLOCKS AND HERDS

1. PALES AND THE PARILIA

PALES was a pastoral deity whose festival took place on the twenty-first of April. Whether the divinity was god or goddess is not known. The day of the festival has been celebrated both in ancient and in modern times as the anniversary of the founding of Rome. Fairly detailed accounts of both the rural and the urban Parilia have come down to us.[1] In the former we note the decoration of the sheep-folds with green branches, the making of fires of straw, laurel, and olive branches through which the flocks were driven and the shepherds leaped, an offering of milk and cakes to Pales, a meal which the worshippers shared with the deity, and a prayer asking forgiveness for any inadvertent offense and also for the safety, health, and increase of the flocks. The urban festival, as celebrated on the Palatine, had similar features, especially notable being the purifi-

---

[1] Ovid, *Fasti,* IV. 721 ff.

catory fires through which the people leaped. The fires were of straw but on them was thrown a mixture of the blood of the October horse sacrificed on the fifteenth of October and the ashes of the unborn calves of the Fordicidia (April 15).

In the decoration of the sheep-folds we have a custom that has survived in the almost universal practice of decoration at special seasons like harvest and Christmas.[2] Fowler's [3] suggestion that the intention was to influence the powers of vegetation is hardly applicable to the Parilia. He is, however, right in pointing out [4] that the prayer and all its concomitant features as described by Ovid survive in the prayer of the peasant of the Roman Campagna today: the pagan shepherd turned to the east, wet his hands with dew, and addressed to Pales the supplication the content of which has been indicated above; the modern shepherd, although he addresses the Madonna instead of Pales, prays for substantially the same things, and like his pagan prototype turns to the east and uses holy water.

[2] Mannhardt, *Antike Wald- und Feld-kulte*, 310.
[3] *R. F.*, 81.
[4] *Op. cit.*, 82.

Whether there is still another survival of the Parilia in St. George's Day as celebrated by the herdsmen of eastern Europe is doubtful. To be sure, the Esthonians are accustomed to drive their cattle to pasture for the first time on St. George's Day (April 23), and the same is true of Ruthenians, Bulgarians, and natives of Little Russia.[5] But in all probability this practice is a survival of an ancient custom similar to the Parilia rather than a relic of the Parilia itself.

2. FAUNUS AND THE LUPERCALIA

THE Lupercalia, which fell on the fifteenth of February, was one of the most ancient festivals in Rome. With what divinity it was originally associated is uncertain. Ovid,[6] it is true, refers to a connection with the rustic god Faunus, but this may have been a later development. The celebration took place at the foot of the Palatine Hill, the site of the earliest Roman settlement, and was characterized by certain notable features. The ceremonies began with a sacrifice of goats and a dog and an offering of

[5] Frazer, *Golden Bough*, II. 330 ff. This work is referred to as *G. B.*, and citations are from the third edition, unless otherwise stated.

[6] *Fasti*, II. 268; V. 101.

sacred cakes furnished by the Vestals. Then two youths, the leaders of two groups of Luperci (as the priests of the rite were called), had their foreheads smeared with the knife that had been used in the sacrifice and then wiped off with wool dipped in milk, whereupon they were expected to laugh. Next the two bands of Luperci, led by the youths just mentioned, naked except for goatskins about their loins, ran around the boundaries of the Palatine, and as they ran they struck with strips cut from the hides of the victims all the women who came in their way.

Into the explanation of the different features of the festival it is not necessary to enter here. No entirely satisfactory interpretation of all parts of the ceremony has ever been offered, although many theories have been advanced.[7] The circumambulation of the Palatine Hill by the two companies of runners seems to indicate a ritual purification of the original site of the city. The striking of the women with the strips of hide shows that at some time or other the idea of fertilization became an important part of the ceremonial complex.

[7] The most important discussions are listed by Frazer in his *Fasti of Ovid*, Vol. II. p. 328.

It was one of the most popular of all the pagan festivals, and it was on its celebration on the fifteenth of February in 44 B.C., a month before his assassination, that Julius Caesar was offered a crown by Antony. It lasted longer than any other Roman festival. It was celebrated long after Christianity had been established and was only suppressed by Pope Gelasius I in A.D. 494.

It has often been said [8] that when Pope Gelasius suppressed the Lupercalia, he instituted the Feast of the Purification of the Virgin, celebrated on the second of February and called Candlemas from the candles and tapers carried in the procession. But this is a mistake. The Christian festival appears to be of other than Roman origin, and it seems clear that it was not introduced into Rome till about A.D. 700.[9] Nevertheless there is a connection between the Lupercalia and Candlemas. A festival stressing purification as the latter did and also occurring in February, the month long associated through the Lupercalia with the idea of purification, made a double appeal to the

[8] Fowler, *R. F.*, 321; Frazer, *Fasti of Ovid*, Vol. II. p. 328.
[9] Usener, *Weihnachtsfest*, 318; Barns in *E. R. E.*, III. 190.

people and so found ready acceptance among them. Moreover the relation to women, which is so notable a feature of the pagan festival, has appeared also in some modern celebrations of Candlemas. In the north of England it used to be called " The Wives' Feast Day."

An interesting analogue to the striking of the women by the Luperci is found in some festivals of modern Europe. For example in the Upper Palatinate the bride is struck with willow or birch twigs as she walks up from the church door to the place where the marriage service is to be read.[10]

It is probable also that the Lupercalia was one of the festivals that contributed something to that spirit of license that has always characterized the mediaeval and modern Carnival.[11] That the latter does not go back to any one Roman festival seems likely. It is of mixed origin. And while, as will be seen later, the Saturnalia was an important influence in its development, the Lupercalia and possibly other festivals also played their part in it.

[10] Hartland, *Primitive Paternity*, I. 105.
[11] See pp. 67 ff.

VI. GODS OF AGRICULTURE

1. CERES AND THE CEREALIA

ON THE nineteenth of April, the day of the festival of Ceres (Cerealia), foxes were let loose in the Circus Maximus with burning brands tied to their brushes. The significance of this practice is uncertain. Ceres [1] was an old Latin deity of the productive powers of the earth but was afterwards identified with the Greek Demeter. Whether the foxes belong to the original festival or are due to Greek influence it is not possible to say. Their reddish color is perhaps an element in the question and has been connected by Preller [2] with the rust to which the grain is subject at this time of year and by Wissowa [3] with the fiery heat of the sun. That the ceremony had something to do with the prosperity of the crops seems certain.

[1] The name Ceres is probably derived from the root of *creare*.

[2] Preller-Jordan, *Röm. Myth.*, II. 43.

[3] *R. u. K.*, 197.

There are some apparent survivals of the practice. Brand [4] quotes a statement from an earlier writer [5] to the effect that in Elgin and the shire of Murray farmers carry burning torches around their crops in the middle of June " in memory of the Cerealia." A similar custom prevailed in Northumberland during the first half of the nineteenth century, when fire-brands used to be carried about the fields on the night of the twenty-ninth of June.

For the connection of Ceres with the festival of the Ambarvalia, see under Mars, page 48.

2. ROBIGUS AND THE ROBIGALIA

ROBIGUS was the spirit of mildew, whose hostility to the growing crops it was the purpose of the festival on the twenty-fifth of April (Robigalia) to avert. Whether this divinity was masculine (Robigus) or feminine (Robigo) has never been definitely ascertained. We have, however, data in regard to the festival.[6] A procession was organized in Rome which, leaving the city by the Porta Flaminia, crossed the Milvian Bridge and proceeded to a grove of

---

[4] *Op. cit.,* I. 310.
[5] Shaw in Appendix II to Pennant's Tour.
[6] Ovid, *Fasti,* IV. 901 ff.

Robigus at the fifth milestone on the Via
Claudia. There the *exta* of a dog and sheep,
which had been killed in the city in the morning, were offered to the divinity. This milestone was doubtless the limit of Roman terri-
tory when the ceremony was first instituted,
and the benefit of procession, prayer, and sacrifice was supposed to extend to all the crops
within the boundaries.

Connected with the Robigalia but distinct
from it was another ceremony consisting of a
sacrifice of red puppies. Unlike the Robigalia
this was a movable festival. Moreover, it took
place not on the Via Claudia but near one of
the city gates, which indeed derived its name
(Porta Catularia) from the ceremony. The
color of the dogs sacrificed on this occasion has
been interpreted in the same way as that of the
foxes at the Cerealia.[7]

Of this ancient ceremony we have record of
an interesting survival in the Litania Maior, or
Romana, of the Catholic Church on St. Mark's
Day, the very day of the Roman Robigalia
(April 25).[8] Like the pagan ceremony this in-

[7] See above, p. 42.

[8] Duchesne, *op. cit.*, 288; Mershman in *Catholic Encyclopaedia*, IX. 287; Lanciani, *Pagan and Christian Rome*,
164.

cluded a procession and prayers. The procession, starting from San Lorenzo in Lucina, held a station at San Valentino outside the Walls and another at the Milvian Bridge. Then, instead of proceeding along the Via Claudia as the old Roman procession had done, it turned to the left and after stopping at a station of the Holy Cross went on to St. Peter's Basilica.[9] This litany was later discontinued but its purpose was obviously the same as that of the pagan ceremony, namely, to gain the blessing of heaven for the crops.

3. FLORA AND THE FLORALIA

FLORA was one of the divinities of the old Roman system. Her function, as her name indicates, manifested itself in blossom. Of her antiquity we have adequate evidence in the well-attested existence of a *flamen* attached to her service (*flamen Floralis*).[10] Possibly she was ultimately of Sabine origin and was a representative of the Sabine element in early Roman religion. The month in the Sabine calendar that corresponds to July is thought to derive its

[9] The ceremony is described in the *Liber Pontificalis*, in the life of Leo III (795–816).

[10] Cf. Varro, *L. L.*, VII. 45.

name from her. Moreover, the oldest temple of Flora of which we have record was in the Sabine quarter of the city on the Quirinal Hill.[11] The fact that the festival is not designated in capital letters on the stone calendars, as is customary in the case of the oldest festivals, may be due to its having been originally a movable feast. We are told that games were first celebrated in her honor about 238 B.C.[12] This was done in accordance with an oracle of the Sibylline Books which had been consulted on the occasion of a famine. We know that a temple was dedicated to her in 238 and that the day of dedication was April 28.[13] It is possible that this was the day of the old Italic festival although the games, especially after they became annual in 173 B.C., contained many Greek features, some of which were due to the points of contact between the cults of Flora and Aphrodite.

The festival was notorious for its license. Among other things it was one of the feast-days of the prostitutes of the city. Moreover, among the gifts distributed were medallions whose ob-

[11] Cf. Steuding in Roscher's *Lexikon,* under Flora.

[12] This is Pliny's date, *N. H.,* XVIII. 29. 3. 286; Velleius I. 14 gives 241 B.C.

[13] Cf. Aust, *De aedibus sacris pop. Rom.,* 17.

scene content obviously pertained to the idea of
fertilization. Beans and lupines were also scat-
tered among the populace and it seems likely
that these were not merely largesses of food.
They were symbols of fertility,[14] and to this
practice we have something analogous in our
custom of throwing rice at weddings. It can
hardly be said, however, that the latter is a survival of the former. As Mannhardt [15] and
Frazer [16] have shown, customs of this kind have
prevailed among many peoples and the data
seem to indicate that our practice is only a parallel. The same is true of the relation to the
Floralia of some of the features of the Gypsy
spring festival on St. George's Day (April 23)
— " Green George " as he is called — as well as
some of the characteristics of May-day festivities. Such resemblances as exist between
these ancient and modern celebrations should
in all likelihood be attributed to the general
similarity to be found among many festivals
celebrated by different peoples at this time
of year.

[14] Cf. Mannhardt, *Kind. u. Korn*, 351 ff.
[15] *Loc. cit.*
[16] *G. B.*, passim.

4. MARS AND THE AMBARVALIA

THE Ambarvalia was celebrated at the end of
May (about the twenty-ninth), and consisted
chiefly of a procession in which the victims of
the threefold sacrifice — pig, sheep, and bull —
were driven thrice around the fields. It was
one of several ceremonies of purification of the
same type. Another was the Amburbium (February 2), in which the procession passed around
the sacred boundary of the city; in another the
victims were driven around an assembly of
citizens on the Campus Martius; in another
around the bounds of a district (*pagus*); and
in another around a single farm. The lustration festival held by the Fratres Arvales in
May has not been specifically included in the
list because there is a strong probability of its
being identical with the Ambarvalia.[17] Originally the triple sacrifice was to Mars,[18] although
by Augustus' time it was made to Ceres [19] and
the extant records of the Arval Brothers refer
to the Dea Dia as the divinity honored. A long

[17] Mommsen, Henzen, Jordan and Wissowa are of this
opinion. Fowler inclines to it but does not think that
Marquardt's doubts are to be wholly disregarded.

[18] Cf. Cato, *De agric.*, 141.

[19] Virgil, *Georgics*, I. 338 ff.

inscription in the Umbrian dialect describes similar ceremonies at the city of Iguvium (now Gubbio), with circumambulating processions and sacrifice of victims.[20]

The purpose of the Ambarvalia was to gain the favor of the gods for the growing crops, and the festival has survived down to our own time. In Italy on the Rogation days before Ascension priests lead their parishioners around the fields and with the Litania Minor [21] invoke the divine blessing on their households and their crops. Some modifications are of course inevitable, but there is a striking similarity between the content of the Christian and the pagan prayer. Trede, who published his work in 1889, states that he has seen in southern Italy processions of the Ambarvalia type in which even animals (lambs and calves) appeared.[22] These, vowed to the Saint in whose honor the procession was held, were afterwards sold, the money being used for the benefit of the sanctuary. Among the places which Trede mentions as the scene of such a ceremony are San Giorgio at the foot of Vesuvius, where two fat calves, adorned

[20] Cf. Buck, *A Grammar of Oscan and Umbrian,* 260 ff.
[21] Mershman in *Catholic Encyclopaedia,* IX. 287.
[22] *Op. cit.,* II. 43.

with ribbons and garlands, formed part of the procession; Pagani (not far from Pompeii), where the offering, which was made to the Madonna, consisted of fowls; and villages in Calabria where goats, pigs, and bullocks, decked like the animals in the Roman Ambarvalia, were led to the sanctuary of the local Saint. For the town of Angri, in the neighborhood of Pompeii, an interesting custom is reported. For there, if by chance drought occurred in summer or excessive rain in winter, a statue of St. John the Baptist was carried about the fields in the belief that he would restore normal conditions. This ceremony was followed by a festive meal in which Trede sees a survival of the banquet mentioned by Tibullus [23] in his account of a purification of the fields in the time of Augustus. There is a resemblance, but it is not at all certain that the festival referred to by Tibullus was the Ambarvalia. It may have been the Feriae Sementivae held late in January.[24]

Fowler, writing in 1899,[25] describes a similar ceremony as still observed in some parishes in England on one of the three days before Ascen-

[23] II. 1. 21–30.
[24] Cf. K. F. Smith, *Elegies of Tibullus,* 391.
[25] *R. F.,* 127. Cf. also Brand, *op. cit.,* I. 202.

sion Day. The minister, the church officials, and parishioners pass in procession around the boundaries of the parish and pray for a blessing on the products of the farms and for the safety of the parish. This was called " beating the bounds." Fowler mentions specifically the celebration of this ceremony at Oxford, although from his account the practice there seems to be somewhat in decline. Apparently the lustration procession that used to be held at Charlton-on-Otmoor near Oxford, on Mayday, has been given up. But till comparatively recent times it was the practice there to carry in procession through the parish a cross decorated with flowers. Similar processions in which the cross is carried are reported for Holland and other parts of the Continent.

Traces of this old custom are found in America also. German Lutherans living in the neighborhood of Fox Lake in southern Wisconsin used to celebrate a sort of Ambarvalia.[26] Farmers and their wives walked around the boundaries of their lands, sprinkling salt and offering prayers for the growing crops. This was on Ascension Day in May. Although the

[26] I am indebted to Miss Ann Gallagher, a student at the University of Chicago, for this example.

record furnished refers to a period some twenty-five years ago, it is possible that the custom still obtains in some places. The Catholics in the neighborhood held processions of the same kind, the prayers used being Pater Noster and Ave Maria.

Of the ceremony at the Umbrian city of Iguvium, described in the famous inscription of the Iguvine Tables, there may be traces in the processional rite celebrated annually on May 15 in the town of Gubbio, which now occupies this site. The connection, however, has never been clearly demonstrated. For while a procession forms the dominating feature of both ceremonies, there is no similarity of purpose. The ancient ceremony was for the lustration of the people and the place; the modern is chiefly in honor of S. Ubaldo, whose monastery on the hill above the town is the objective of the procession of the Ceri which passes through the streets. Nor can we be sure that the word Ceri — pedestals surmounted by figures of Saints — is related to Cerfus Martius who is mentioned as a local deity in the ancient inscription.[27]

[27] Bower, *The Elevation and Procession of the Ceri;* McCracken, *Gubbio, Past and Present.*

5. Consus and the Consualia

Consus (from *condere,* to store) was the god
of harvest. Tertullian [28] tells us that there was
a sacrifice to him on the seventh of July at his
underground altar in the Circus Maximus.
From the stone calendars and other sources
we know that a festival in his honor, the Consualia, was celebrated on the twenty-first of
August and on the fifteenth of December.
There was also another ceremony that was
connected with his worship, namely, the Opi-
consivia on the twenty-fifth of August.

The fact that the sacrifice to Consus falls on
the same day as the Festival of Handmaids
(Feriae Ancillarum), the seventh of July, may
be a coincidence without significance. It is
possible, however, that there is a connection
between the two, and that the bizarre antics of
the maids were one form of harvest festivities.
On this day [29] the slave girls (*ancillae*) sacrificed beneath a wild fig-tree (*caprificus*),
dressed themselves in their mistresses' clothes,
and ran about striking one another with
branches and pelting each other with stones.

[28] *De spectaculis,* 5.
[29] The day was called Nonae Caprotinae.

Moreover, they railed with unbridled license at any one passing by. It was maids' day out in the widest sense of the term. It is in their attitude toward persons passing by that Fowler [30] sees a possible connection between their festival and harvest celebrations. He cites as a parallel the rough treatment accorded in many parts of Europe to strangers appearing in the fields at harvest-time, some of whom are tied up in straw and only released on paying ransom, while others are made to submit to a ducking. He makes special reference to the survival of this custom in Derbyshire where the stranger in the field is still made " to pay his footing."

The Consualia celebrated on the twenty-first of August was a harvest-home festival. There were horse-races and mule-races, and the tradition that it was on the occasion of this festival that the rape of the Sabine women took place, in its implication of the presence of strangers from other communities, furnishes some indication of the scale of the celebration. The legend points also to sexual license as one of the characteristics of harvest celebrations.

[30] *R. F.*, 177.

6. MARS AND THE OCTOBER HORSE

ONE other ceremony apparently connected with the harvest should be mentioned. This was the annual sacrifice of a horse on the fifteenth of October. On that day there was a race of two-horse chariots on the Campus Martius, and after the race the near horse of the winning team was sacrificed to Mars at his ancient altar on the Campus. The head of the horse was cut off and, after being adorned with cakes, was fought for by the inhabitants of two of the regions of Rome, the Sacred Way and the Subura. If the former were victorious they fastened it up on the Regia in the Forum; if the latter won, they fixed it on a tower [31] in their part of the town. The horse's tail also was cut off and taken to the Regia where the blood from it dripped on the hearth. Although the significance of these parts of the ceremony has been the subject of much discussion, it seems probable that they involve the familiar religious idea of the continuance of fertility from year to year and so tend to confirm the classification of the rite as a harvest festival. The decoration of the horse's head with cakes

[31] Turris Mamilia.

inevitably recalls the similar adornment of the horses and mules at the Consualia and other agricultural celebrations. And there is also the statement of Paulus [32] that the rite was " on account of the harvest." Fundamentally this theory rests on the assumption that the ceremony goes back to a time when Mars was thought of as a vegetation-spirit and had not yet become specialized in men's minds as a god of war. Wissowa [33] rejects this explanation, and denying any connection of the rite with the harvest contends that from the beginning it was celebrated in honor of Mars as war-god and marked the conclusion of the year's campaigns. In his opinion the horse was a war-horse. His arguments, however, are not convincing.

At present it is the fashion among students of comparative religion to disparage the " corn-spirit " which explained so much to the scholars of the last generation. Probably the theory was applied with too little discrimination. But it is in the main sound, and in all likelihood the explanation of the October horse is to be found here.

[32] Page 277 (edition of Thewrewk de Ponor), *ob frugum eventum.*

[33] *R. u. K.,* 143.

Of this mid-October rite it is not possible to mention any specific survival in modern times. But it is not without pertinence to draw attention to the October festival held by the peasants of the Roman Campagna today. Moreover, the examples cited by Mannhardt[34] and Frazer[35] of horses and other animals appearing as the corn-spirit in modern cultures, although not survivals of the Roman rite, none the less find their ultimate origin in a class of ancient religious ideas of which the ceremony of the October horse was one local manifestation. In the same way the fundamental idea involved in the fight for the horse's head between the men of the Sacred Way and those of the Subura still persists in such contests as Frazer[36] enumerates. And to the fastening of the head on a building many parallels are given by Mannhardt,[37] Frazer,[38] and Fowler:[39] a sheaf of grain, a bunch of flowers, or the effigy of some animal, in some cases that of a horse.

[34] *Mythologische Forschungen*, 156 ff.
[35] *G. B.*, VII. 292 ff.
[36] *Op. cit.*, VII. 75 ff.
[37] *A. W. F.*, 214 ff.
[38] *Op. cit.*, VIII. 44.
[39] *R. F.*, 246.

7. SATURN AND THE SATURNALIA

THE festival of Saturn fell on December 17, but its popular celebration lasted for seven days. It began as a country festival in the time when agriculture was one of the chief activities of the Romans, but it soon came to be celebrated in urban centers also. It was a period of indulgence in eating, drinking, and gambling, and during these seven days city officials condoned conduct that they would not have tolerated at any other season. One feature of the occasion was the license allowed to slaves, who were permitted to treat their masters as if they were their social equals.[40] Frequently indeed masters and slaves changed places and the latter were waited on by the former. Another feature of the celebration was the exchange of gifts, such as candles (*cerei*) which are supposed to have symbolized the increasing power of the sunlight after the winter solstice,[41] and little puppets of paste or earthenware (*sigillaria*), the exact significance of which is obscure. It was a season of hilarity and good-will, and

[40] Accius, quoted by Macrobius, *Sat.*, I. 7. 37; Horace, *Sat.*, II. 7. 5.
[41] Fowler, *R. F.*, 272.

the universal greeting was " Bona Saturnalia! "
A " king " was chosen by lot, who would bid
one of his subjects dance, another sing, another
carry a flute-girl on his back and so forth.[42]
In this play-king the Romans ridiculed royalty.

Frazer's [43] attempt to reconstruct the king
of the Roman Saturnalia on the basis of the
martyrdom of St. Dasius at Durostolum on the
Danube in A.D. 303 is ingenious but untenable.
The story of Dasius is told in a Greek manu-
script in the Bibliothèque Nationale.[44] According to this source the Roman soldiers at
Durostolum were in the habit of celebrating the
Saturnalia with a human sacrifice. Thirty days
before the festival they chose by lot a handsome
youth whom they arrayed as king and who, as
the representative of good king Saturn, was attended by a brilliant escort and given full license to indulge in any pleasure. But on the
thirtieth day he was obliged to kill himself on
the altar of the god Saturn whom he was per-
sonating. In 303 the lot fell to a Christian sol-

[42] Tacitus, *Ann.*, XIII. 15, where Nero was " king " and
seized the opportunity to humiliate Britannicus; also Seneca,
Apoc., 8 and *Ep.*, 47. 14; Epictetus, *Diss.*, I. 25. 8; and
Lucian, *Saturn.*, 4.
[43] *G. B.*, II. 310 f.; IX. 310 ff.
[44] Cf. Cumont, *Revue de Philologie*, XXI, 143 ff. (1897).

dier, Dasius, who, refusing to play a part that involved a month of immorality, was beheaded on the twentieth of November.[45] Frazer sees in this practice at Durostolum a survival of the original form of the festival and regards the innocuous king of the Saturnalia, of whom Roman writers speak, as merely a faint adumbration of a personage of much more tragic experience. But the theory will not hold. For while there seems no adequate reason for doubting, as Wissowa [46] does, the historicity of the Dasius story, its features (especially the human sacrifice) strongly suggest the influence of Oriental rites.[47] It seems certain, indeed, that the king of the festival celebrated at Durostolum was some one quite other than the king of the Roman Saturnalia, who was never anything more than a merry-making master of revels.

To be sure the festival suffered the usual legendary accretions. From being the holiday of country folk in a slack season of the year, it came to be thought of as symbolic of the

[45] Reinach, *Cultes, Mythes et Religions,* I. 332 ff.

[46] In Roscher, *Lexikon,* IV. 440, and *R. u. K.,* 207.

[47] Reinach, *op. cit.,* 334 ff.; Fowler, *The Religious Experience of the Roman People* (referred to in this book as *R. E.*), 112; Nilsson in Pauly-Wissowa, *Real-Encyclopädie,* II A. 208.

golden age when Saturn had been king of
Latium, when all men were equal, when there
was no labor, and when life was a continual
round of pleasure. And in this interpretation
of it the king of the revels personified old King
Saturn. But a satisfactory analysis of the different elements in the festival has never been
made. It is known that it was subjected to
Greek influence but it is difficult to distinguish
precisely between original and acquired characteristics. Moreover, in any study of it that
is undertaken it must be remembered that
many peoples have had and in some cases still
have a similar festival at this time of year.
And the similarity of the conditions that occasion the festival — whether it be the leisure
period of the farmer's year or the recognition
of the new solar year that begins after the winter solstice, or both — may easily result in the
independent development in different communities of analogous forms of celebration.

There are interesting survivals of the Saturnalia in some of the customs of our Christmas
and New Year's holidays, in the Carnival, and
in the festivities of Shrove Tuesday. These
will now be discussed under their respective
heads.

(1) CHRISTMAS AND NEW YEAR

THE extremists who have said that Christmas was intended to replace the Saturnalia have vastly overstated the case. Nor is it of any importance that Epiphanius,[48] the bishop of Salamis in Cyprus in the fourth century, places the Saturnalia on the twenty-fifth of December. This is not the only error in the list of dates in which it occurs. Without doubt, however, many of the customs of the Saturnalia were transferred to Christmas. Although the dates did not exactly coincide, for the Saturnalia proper fell on the seventeenth of December, the time of year was practically the same, and it has already been pointed out how frequently festivals of the merry-making type occur among various peoples at this season. Fowler, mentioning the good-will that so generally characterizes these celebrations, raises the question whether this was one of the reasons why Christmas was put at the winter solstice.[49] Possibly, as has also been suggested,[50] the postponement of the festivities from the date of the

[48] *Panar.*, 51.

[49] *R. F.*, 271, note. He cites John Chrysostom III. 497e and Usener, *Religionsgeschichtliche Untersuchungen*, 217.

[50] But cf. Duchesne, *Christian Worship*, 261.

Saturnalia to Christmas week was in part at least caused by the institution of the Advent fast covering the period of the four Sundays before Christmas.

Certainly many of the customs of the Christmas season go back to the Roman festival. In it lies the origin of the excessive eating and drinking, the plethora of sweets, the playing of games, and the exchange of gifts. Nor can we fail to connect our custom of burning candles with the candles (*cerei*) that were so conspicuous a part of the Saturnalia. Moreover, our Christmas holidays, like the Roman festival, are approximately a week. In one part of England at least (North Staffordshire) the farm-servants' annual holiday extends from Christmas to New Year. Nor is this the only point of resemblance to pagan times afforded by the Staffordshire holiday. For the license allowed by masters during its continuance reminds one of the liberties allowed to slaves during the Saturnalia. And there are English hotels at the present time where that inversion of rôle that was one of the features of the Roman festival is practiced at Christmas, and servants and guests change places.

In mediaeval times there were still other survivals, and the king of the Saturnalia is obviously the prototype not only of the Abbot of Unreason who at one time presided over the Christmas revels in Scotland, but also of the Lord of Misrule in England and the Abbé de Liesse in Lille. This mock dignitary had other titles. In some places (Rouen and Evreux) he was called *Abbas Conardorum;* elsewhere he was known as *Rex Stultorum, Facetiarum Princeps, Abbas Iuvenum, Papa Fatuorum,* and *L'Abbé des Foux.* These masters of the revels are all connected with the Feast of Fools (*Festum Fatuorum*) of the mediaeval church, and they masqueraded in clerical vestments. Du Tilliot,[51] in tracing these customs back to the Saturnalia, points out that not only during the celebration of Christmas but through the Feast of Fools or *Festum Kalendarum* (January 1), as it was sometimes called, minor clerics took the place of the superior clergy. The latter festival was indeed notable both for inversion of rôle and for the unbridled conduct of the young priests, who danced in the church, sang obscene songs, played dice during the celebration of the mass, and took part in the theater

[51] In his book *Mémoires à l'histoire de la Fête des Foux.* Cf. also Du Cange, *Glossarium,* under *Kalendae;* and Barns in Hastings, *E. R. E.,* I. 9.

in performances that were disgraced by wanton gestures and immoral lines.

We hear also of the Boy-Bishop (*Episcopus Puerorum*), whose authority lasted from St. Nicholas' day (December 6) till Childermas (December 28) and whose tradition (as well as that of the Bishop of Unreason) still survives to a certain extent in Santa Claus. Apparently the compromise made by the early Church in adapting the customs of the Saturnalia to Christian practice had little or no effect in checking the license of the festival. This continued through the whole Christmas festival and sometimes lasted till the day of Epiphany (January 6). We find many criticisms by churchmen or councils. In England Henry VIII issued a proclamation in 1542, abolishing the revels, but Mary restored them in 1554. The English mummers are said to have worn caps of brown paper, shaped like a miter, and these are traced back either to the Boy Bishops or the Abbots of Misrule. Readers of Sir Walter Scott's novel *The Abbott* [52] will remember the " Right Reverend Abbott of Unreason."

[52] Barns, *loc. cit.*, refers to the historical note in this novel.

There is nothing to be said in support of the theory which Frazer,[53] citing Cumont's [54] account of the Dasius story and Wendland's [55] article, once advanced: namely, that the Saturnalia had originally been celebrated in the spring; that this date was adhered to in some of the outlying parts of the Empire, as at Jerusalem in the time of Pontius Pilate; and that the treatment to which Jesus was subjected — the robe, the crown, the scepter, the mock homage, and the tragic death — finds its explanation in the assumption that he was the king of the Saturnalia as celebrated by the Roman garrison in Jerusalem that year. The improbability of such a theory has been pointed out [56] and the objections to it need not be given in detail here. Frazer [57] himself has practically withdrawn it in his third edition. But unlikely as the theory as a whole is, it brings out one point which deserves careful consideration, and that is the similarity of the mockery of Jesus to that of a king of the Saturnalia. It is in-

[53] *G. B.*, 2d ed., III. 186 ff.

[54] In *Revue de Philologie*, cited above.

[55] " Jesus als Saturnalien-könig," *Hermes*, XXXIII, 175 (1898).

[56] Andrew Lang in *Magic and Religion*, 79 ff.

[57] *G. B.*, IX. 412 ff.

deed probable that the Roman soldiers were
influenced in their conduct by their recollec-
tion of the practices of the Saturnalia in which
they had often taken part. Ridicule of this
kind was probably not uncommon. At any rate
Wendland in the article already referred to has
commented on the resemblance between the
mockery of Jesus and that to which the Jewish
king, Agrippa I, was subjected by the Alexan-
drians in A.D. 38.[58] Moreover, the treatment of
Jesus seems to have followed lines already familiar to the people through the mimes pro-
duced at the Saturnalia as well as at other seasons. For mockery of the burlesque king as
well as of the Jew was common in the mimes
of the period.

(2) THE CARNIVAL

But survivals of the Saturnalia are not confined to Christmas festivities. In spite of the
difference in time of year they are found also
in the Carnival as celebrated in Catholic
countries today. The Abbé de Liesse of Lille,
whose relation to the king of the Saturnalia has
been indicated, presided at games celebrated at
Arras and neighboring towns during the Car-

[58] Reich, in *N. Jahrb. f. klass. Altert.*, XIII, 730 (1904).

nival. Moreover, many of the special features
of the Saturnalia recur in the merry-making of
the Carnival. The confetti used so lavishly are
a relic of the grains of wheat or barley which
to the Romans represented the hope of a year
of abundance. The pointed " fool's cap " of
the Carnival mummer reproduces the liberty
cap which in accordance with the custom of in-
verted rôles slaves were allowed to wear during
the pagan holiday. And the spirit of untram-
meled mockery, hilarity, jesting, and mischief,
so characteristic of the Carnival, is an inheritance from the Roman festival.

(3) SHROVE TUESDAY

THE festivities of Shrove Tuesday, the last day
of the Carnival, as organized by the primitive
Church were notably of the Saturnalian type.
Many examples indicating the degree of license
are recorded.[59] It has been suggested [60] that
the Holly-boy and Ivy-girl, as they appear in
the folklore of Kent,[61] are connected with the

[59] Cf. Dekker, *Seven Deadly Sinnes of London* (1606);
Brand, *op. cit.*, I. 63 ff.

[60] *E. R. E.*, XI. 479.

[61] Brand, *op. cit.*, I. 68, quotes a description of the
burning of a Holly-boy and Ivy-girl on the Tuesday before
Shrove Tuesday in 1779.

German Fastnachtsmann or Prinz Karneval
and so ultimately with the king of the Saturnalia. This connection, however, has never
been adequately established. We may also
consider the possibility of affinity between the
Holly-boy and Ivy-girl of Kent and the Roman
divinities, Liber and Libera, whose festival
(Liberalia) was celebrated on the seventeenth
of March. On this day old women sat in the
streets of Rome, their heads decked with ivy,
and sold cakes (*liba*) of oil and honey.[62] That
the pancakes still so commonly eaten in England on Shrove Tuesday — sometimes called
" Pancake Tuesday " — go back to the cakes
of the Roman Liberalia has been suggested but
never satisfactorily demonstrated.

For the possibility of other Roman festivals
having influenced the Carnival, see under
Lupercalia, p. 41.

[62] Ovid, *Fasti*, III. 725 ff.; Varro, *L. L.*, VI. 14.

VII. ANCIENT RIVER–SPIRITS AND MEDIAEVAL DEVILS

RIVERS of ancient Italy had their spirits. We hear specifically of the god of the river Clitumnus in Umbria, and also of one for the Numicus, a stream in Latium, for the Sebethus [1] near Naples, and for the Po. Curiously enough there is no specific reference to a god of the Tiber in the early period, but possibly the divinity of this river, as Mommsen suggests, is concealed under the name of Volturnus, from *volvere*, with reference to its rolling waters. The latter was one of the indigenous gods of Rome, of whose *flamen* we have record and whose festival, the Volturnalia, is set down in the old calendar for the twenty-seventh of August. The name Tiberinus does not appear in the cult till much later. But these are only a few examples of what must have been a widespread religious practice. We may safely assume that every

[1] *C. I. L.*, X. 1480.

river in ancient Italy was believed to have its god.

This being the case, it is obvious that the building of a bridge always involved the fear of offending the tutelary spirit of the stream and necessitated the undertaking of ceremonies calculated to placate his anger. In many cases the ceremony doubtless took the form of a sacrifice. There may have been such a sacrifice when the Pons Sublicius, the oldest of the bridges across the Tiber, was built. And it has been suggested that the ceremony of the Argei, in which straw puppets were thrown from the bridge into the river, finds its ultimate explanation in an original sacrifice of human beings offered to the god of the river in expiation of the nullification or at least the infringement of his divinity in building a bridge over his waters.[2] This, however, is only a suggestion and the ceremony of the Argei presents so many difficulties of interpretation that definite statements in regard to it are hazardous in the extreme. But it is in connection with propitiatory ceremonies of some sort that we look for the explanation of the term *pontifex* (from *pons*, bridge, and *facio*, make) applied to the members of the ancient

[2] Cf. G. A. Frank Knight in Hastings, *E. R. E.*, II. 848.

college of priests that was most closely associated with the rites of the oldest order of Roman divinities.

This Roman belief in the offense to deity implicit in the building of a bridge is illustrated by examples, similar but of independent origin, found among other peoples. There is a legend that the security of London Bridge was due to its stones having been sprinkled with the blood of children. Another version makes the security of the bridge depend on the sacrifice of a prisoner; and the children's singing game

> *London Bridge is broken down*
> *London Bridge is broken down*
> *London Bridge is broken down*
> My *fair lady*

probably goes back to this form of the belief. For in the game the children seize a prisoner who is released only after a forfeit has been exacted.[3]

In some of the later religious systems the river-spirit of the ancients survived in the form of the Devil. It is said that the Mohammedans of Herzegovina regard a bridge as evi-

[3] Cf. Gomme, *Traditional Games of England, Scotland and Ireland*.

dence of an unholy compact between its builder and the Evil One. Only on the assumption that the Devil has received adequate compensation can they account for the diminution of his power indicated by the bridging of the stream, and so they curse both bridge and builder as they pass.[4] In Christian sects also the Devil succeeded the pagan river-spirit. The appellation " Devil's Bridge " found in so many parts of the world goes back to this ancient heathen idea, for the drift of the legends is that the Devil would not allow the bridge to be built till he had been placated by a human sacrifice.

The pagan associations of bridges survived in still another form in mediaeval Christianity, namely, in the bridge over the river of death in the lower world. All the dread implications of bridge legends and beliefs were intensified in the case of this " Bridge of Death " or " Bridge of Judgment " as it was variously called. For over it the soul must pass.[5] Moreover, a bridge has a conspicuous part in the mediaeval legends of Alberic, St. Paul, and others, as well as in that funeral chant, the " Lyke-Wake Dirge," which was sung in Yorkshire as late as the

[4] Evans, *Through Bosnia and Herzegovina*, 316.
[5] *St. Patrick's Purgatory* (Wright's edition, 1844), chap. 4.

seventeenth century. Whether the appearance of this bridge in the legends of American Indians is due to original native ideas or is to be attributed to their early contacts with Catholic peoples is uncertain.[6]

[6] See G. A. Frank Knight, *loc. cit.*

VIII. PHALLICISM

PHALLICISM had its place among the early cults of Rome and Italy. This is apparent from the existence on the Velia of the shrine of the divinity Mutunus-Tutunus, whose double name has reference to the two sexes. Matrons, closely veiled, made offerings to him, and he played an important part at weddings.[1] Further, the Liberalia, the festival of Ceres and Liber, especially as celebrated at Lavinium, was known far and wide for the prominence of the phallic element, which in all probability antedated the identification of Liber with Dionysus. The cult of Priapus also, a god of procreation and fruitfulness from Lampsacus and other cities on the Hellespont, had reached Italy, and his statue with sickle, club, and phallic symbol, was frequently placed in Roman gardens. Amulets in phallic forms were believed to have power to avert the evil eye and

---

[1] Tertullian, *Apol.*, 25; *Ad nat.*, II. 11. Augustine identifies him with Priapus, *Civ. Dei*, IV. 11, 34. See Wissowa, *R. u. K.*, 169.

for this reason one was fastened to the car of a Roman general celebrating a triumph. Many phallic ex-votos have been found on excavated sites.

Phallic beliefs did not pass away with paganism. A contemporary account of the celebration of the feast of S. Cosma and S. Damiano at Isernia in the Abruzzi in 1780 shows the survival of pagan practices in an amazing degree of detail.[2] These Saints seem to have had in popular belief precisely the position held by Mutunus-Tutunus and Priapus in the minds of the Romans. They were petitioned by those desiring children or seeking a cure for sexual disease, and the offerings made to them were wax models of the parts affected. In France and Belgium during the Middle Ages there were Saints of the same kind. We hear of St. Foutin [3] at Varailles in Provence, from the ceiling of whose chapel many wax ex-votos of phallic form were suspended. In the north of France there was a cult of one Guerlichon or

[2] A letter from Sir William Hamilton, British Minister to the Court of Naples, printed in Payne Knight's book on the *Worship of Priapus*. Cf. Dulaure, *Des divinités generatrices*, 257.

[3] Sometimes called Photin or Foustin. See Hartland, *Primitive Paternity*, I, 63–64.

Greluchon, whose powers were supposed to be
similar to those of Saints Foutin and Cosma.
In Antwerp the figure of one Ters formerly
stood at the gateway to the Church of St. Wal-
burga in the Rue des Pêcheurs.[4] The efforts of
the Church, apparently without effect in the
Middle Ages, have been more successful in our
own times, and the most flagrant abuses have
been stopped. Yet traces of the old beliefs still
linger in the common use by Italians today of
amulets of phallic shape to protect them against
the evil eye. Some of the finger gestures made
for the same purpose are also of phallic origin.

[4] Hartland, *loc. cit.*

IX. THE WORSHIP OF THE SPIRITS OF THE DEAD

A CULT of the spirits of the dead was one of the phases of Roman religion.[1] In February (from the thirteenth to the twenty-first) there was a celebration of rites at the tombs of deceased members of the family. The festival was called Parentalia (from *parens*, parent, ancestor) and offerings were made to the deified shades of the departed. That the spirits of the dead were thought of as gods is shown by the custom which Plutarch,[2] citing Varro, mentions, namely, that when the sons on cremating the body of their father first saw the bones freed from the flesh they called out that the dead had become a god. There is also the letter of Cornelia to her son, in which she speaks of the divinity that would be hers after death.[3] Moreover, the spirits of the dead

[1] Fragment of Twelve Tables in Cic., *Leg.*, II. 9. 22: Deorum manium iura sancta sunto; suos leto datos divos habento.

[2] *Quaest. Rom.*, 14.

[3] Cornelius Nepos, Frag. 2 (Winstedt's edition, Oxford,

were regularly called *di manes* (the good gods).[4] The epithet *manes* was euphemistic and its purpose was to placate them.

One of the elements in the attitude of the Romans toward the dead was the hope that through the performance of the prescribed ceremonies and the making of offerings they would win their favor and assistance; with their aid, they thought, good fortune might be their lot. Virgil brings this out clearly in Aeneas' words at his father's tomb: " Let us ask him for fair winds." [5]

Besides the Parentalia there were two other festivals of the dead, the Larentalia on the twenty-third of December and the Lemuria on the ninth, eleventh, and thirteenth of May. On the occasion of the former an offering was made by the pontiffs and the high-priest of Quirinus at the so-called grave of Larenta in the district of Rome known as the Velabrum. But we know that it was not a grave; it was a *mundus,* that is one of those round pits into

---

1904): ubi mortua ero, parentabis mihi et invocabis deum parentem.

[4] Varro, *L. L.,* VI. 4: bonum antiqui dicebant manum.

[5] *Aeneid,* V. 59–60:

Poscamus ventos, atque haec me sacra quotannis
Urbe velit posita templis sibi ferre dicatis.

which offerings to the gods of the lower world were cast. For it is clearly indicated in many sources that the Romans believed that the spirits of the dead lived beneath the earth. Larenta seems to have been a divinity of the lower world, possibly of Sabine origin.[6] The ceremonies of the May festival, the Lemuria, furnish unmistakable evidence of the belief that the spirits of the dead sometimes revisited their former homes and unless placated would make mischief. At midnight the head of the family walked through the house and, spitting out black beans as an offering to the ghosts, nine times he bade them take their departure.[7]

Mention should also be made of the festival of Rosaria, a private ceremony, celebrated by Roman families or organizations in May. On this occasion tombs were lavishly decorated with roses.

The account given indicates the general nature of Roman eschatological belief. One of its most obvious and notable features is fear, as is seen not only from the euphemism of the appellation *di manes* but also from the ceremonies of the Parentalia and Lemuria. A de-

[6] Varro, *L. L.*, V. 74 (*Larunda*).
[7] Manes exite paterni (Ov., *Fasti*, V. 443).

sire to prevent a hostile attitude on the part of
the spirits is seen everywhere. The performance of the ceremonies and the making of the
offerings were the fulfilment of the just requirements of the divine beings (*ius divinum*).
Neglect of these would result in unfriendly relations with the shades such as pious Romans
could not contemplate with tranquillity. The
fear, to be sure, was vague and indefinite, but
it was none the less efficacious. Vagueness, indeed, is another of the notable characteristics
of the whole cult of the dead. In the early
period and almost to the end of the Republic
there seems to have been little individualiza-
tion of the spirits of the departed. The tendency was to regard them as an indiscriminate
multitude. References to the spirit of a particular individual are more common in the imperial period.[8] When detailed descriptions of
the lower world or definite references to the
felicity of the blessed and the punishment of
the wicked in Hades appear in Latin literature, they are invariably borrowed from
foreign sources. They had no place in the old
Roman religion.

[8] Tacitus, *Ann.*, XIII. 14. 6: infernos Silanorum manes
invocare.

The pagan festivals of the dead seem to have been among those that showed persistence in survival.[9] There are indications that they were celebrated even under Christian emperors. For a list of Campanian festivals approved by the Christian emperor Theodosius in the year 387 includes a festival of the dead held at Lake Avernus. The list occurs in an inscription and it is noticeable that not a single Christian festival is mentioned. Either the number of Christians in Campania at the end of the fourth century was negligible or the Christians participated in pagan rites.

But even after the pagan festivals ceased to be celebrated, the belief that the spirits of the dead could and, if properly approached, would give aid and protection to the living survived. The fathers of the Church saw that this was one of those inherent beliefs to which the people would cling with that unyielding pertinacity that manifests itself in the case of hereditary ideas. They compromised, shifting from the cult of the spirits of ancestors to the veneration of persons whose virtues, sufferings, or miraculous deeds justified their being regarded as intermediaries between God and man.

[9] Cf. Preller-Jordan, *Röm. Myth.*, II. 74.

In other words the Saints succeeded to the worship of the dead just as they succeeded to the cult of the departmental deities and to the "little gods" of the Roman household. What happened in the case of the transfer of the cult of the departmental deities to that of the Saints has already been described. The same thing occurred in the transfer of the cult of ancestors to the Saints. For while the Church never gave the Saints a higher place than that of intermediaries and intercessors whose aid might prove efficacious in gaining the favor of God, the masses of the population made no such fine distinctions, and confusing means and end came to regard the Saints themselves as present helps in trouble and addressed their prayers directly to them. They were more interested in their power to help them in their troubles than in their virtuous lives or harrowing deaths. Prior to the Reformation the efforts to check this tendency toward polytheism took the form of ecclesiastical legislation but this proved ineffectual.

Apart from the general doctrine of the veneration of Saints, there are some specific festivals of the modern Church that go back directly to pagan customs connected with the dead. One of these is All Saints' Day, now celebrated on the first of November but till the time of Pope Gregory III observed on the thirteenth of May, which was one of the days of the Roman festival of the dead, the Lemuria. Whether there is any connection between these dates or not, the rites of All Saints' Day are a survival not of the Lemuria but of the Parentalia. For in the modern festival the faithful visit the tombs of the Saints, venerate their relics, and pray for their blessing. The next day also, the second of November, All Souls' Day, unquestionably reproduces some of the features of the Parentalia. People go in great numbers to the cemeteries and deck the graves of the members of their family with flowers and candles, and the mass, which takes the place of the ancient sacrifice, is directed to the repose of the souls of the departed.

Another survival may be noted here. On the day after the Parentalia and forming a sort of conclusion to it was the festival known as the Caristia or Cara Cognatio (February 22). This was a feast in which the members of the family, after performing their duties to the dead, participated. It seems highly probable that it was one of the contributing influences to the *agape* or love-feast of the primitive Christians.[10]   It was not, however, the sole source of this custom.   Common meals were an established institution among the Jews and were a well-known feature of Roman trade guilds and associations of other kinds.   At first the *agape* was attended by all the members of the congregation rich and poor, and was either preceded or followed by the celebration of the Eucharist.   Later it was separated from the Eucharist and gradually came to be confined to the poor members of the group.   It was the cause of increasing dissension in the fourth century and at length was discontinued.   Vestiges of the custom, however, remained till the Council of Basle in the fifteenth century.   And it has been revived in modern times by some German Baptists, the Moravian Brethren, the Wesleyan Methodists, and in Scotland by the followers of Robert Sandeman.

Of the Lemuria with its prohibition of weddings during the days of its celebration (May 9, 11, 13) we may have a survival in the proverb; " Bad prove the wives that are married in May."

A conspicuous and notable part of the reli-

[10] Cf. Duchesne, *Christian Worship*, 49.

gious ceremonies pertaining to the dead was the funeral procession, which in the case of men prominent on account of their birth or achievements was organized on a highly elaborate scale. Starting from the home of the deceased it passed to the Forum, where it halted for the delivery of the funeral oration, and then proceeded to the family tomb, which was always outside the city-walls and generally on one of the highways. Component parts of the procession were musicians, professional mourners, dancers and clowns, slaves freed by the will of the deceased, carriages in which rode mutes wearing the masks of ancestors, torch-bearers, the funeral bier on which lay the deceased with face exposed, the sons with covered, the daughters with uncovered head, and in some cases painted representations of heroic achievements by land or sea.

An analysis of this procession enables us to reach a reasonable conjecture in regard to the ultimate significance of its different elements. For obviously it is not of single origin. To be sure the desire to do honor to the dead was present in ancient as well as in modern funerals. But the fundamental motive lay deeper, and was intimately associated with the belief of the Romans concerning the relations between the living and the dead. Of one phase of this belief — perhaps the one indicating the lowest spiritual level — we have evidence in the presence of musicians and clowns. For on the analogy of practices common in other cultures the pipers and harlequins were there to counteract the evil influence of either the spirit of the deceased himself or other demons of mischief-making type. The dirge of the professional mourners, with its set content of expression of the grief of the survivors and praise of the merits of the dead, can be traced back to the days when there were no professional mourners and the surviving members of the family sought to appease the spirit of the departed by the double compliment of the manifestation of their inconsolable grief now that he was gone and the description of his high qualities and the recital of his achievements. This same desire to be in good relations with the dead was one of the principal motives also in the extravagant demonstrations of grief sometimes shown by the relatives during the funeral procession, such as tearing of hair, mutilation of face, beating of breast, and rending of garments. Not that the religious motive was always the operative one. Sometimes, it would seem, the funeral hysterics of the survivors had the extremely mundane purpose of averting suspicions of foul play, which were always rife in a society in which poisoning at one time or another had a considerable degree of vogue. The torch-bearers have been explained as going back to the time when funerals were regularly held at night and lights were necessary. But in the employment of the torch in funerals of the historic period and its acceptance as a funerary emblem there is probably more than the remnant of a practical usage. Whether it was believed that the torch served to light the soul to the world beyond or cheer and comfort it or ward off malicious spirits it is difficult to say. Whatever its precise interpretation was, it was firmly established in the ritual of the services for the dead. So far as all the other features of the procession are concerned — the parade of masks of ancestors, the files of manumitted slaves and other retainers, the pictorial representation of military or naval victories — we must recognize that below the desire to pay honor lay that old fear of the spirit of the dead and the uneasy feeling that if one were to expect any measure of success or prosperity in this world, it was essential to avoid the hostility of those who had passed into the next.

Taken over by the Christian Church as early as the fourth century, the funeral procession has come down the ages essentially the same in the general nature of its appeal to the spectators and even retaining, though with changed significance, some of the details of the Roman practice. For example, it is reasonable to assume that the placing of lighted candles near the body of the deceased and the carrying of them in funeral processions is derived from that use of the torch at Roman funerals to which reference has just been made. Moreover, professional mourners are still employed at funerals in Campania and Calabria.

It has been thought that the " Dance of Death," a species of spectacular play that has been traced back to the fourteenth century, shows the influence of the Roman funeral. The resemblance is not striking, though there is some similarity between the ancient funeral march and the Trionfo della Morte as celebrated in Florence in the sixteenth century as part of the Carnival. For in addition to the Christian figure of the Angel blowing the last trump and Death with his scythe there were

men in black and white garb wearing death-
masks as well as singers chanting the " Mise-
rere."

Some scholars have held also that influence
of the Roman funeral procession may be seen
in the " Breton Pardon." But this is doubtful.
The most notable features of that institution
are obviously of different origin.

The custom of the funeral oration was taken
over by the Church. We know that St. Ambrose delivered one in honor of his brother
Satyrus, that St. Jerome spoke in memory of
Paula, and St. Gregory on the occasion of the
death of Basil of Caesarea. The practice has
been continued down to our own times and the
addresses common at funerals or memorial
services in America and elsewhere reproduce
some of the characteristics of the Roman *lau-
datio funebris*.

The custom of adorning the tombs of relatives with roses (the festival of Rosaria) survived the fall of paganism. The early Christians decorated the tombs of martyrs with
evergreens, violets, amaranths, and roses.
Churches also were frequently decked with
flowers on important anniversaries. Moreover, roses and other flowers were often

carved on Christian tombs, and roses are painted on the walls of the catacombs of Calixtus. Later the pagan Rosaria became incorporated in the Christian feast of Pentecost, which the Italians still call the Pasqua Rosa.[11]

Further, the conception of cemeteries as hallowed ground, as it obtains among modern Christian communities, is an inheritance from Roman religion, which from very early times set aside places of burial as *loci sacri*.

[11] Lanciani, *Pagan and Christian Rome*, 50.

X. DIANA AND THE VIRGIN MARY

THE CULT of Diana was of Italian origin and in all probability was introduced into Rome from Aricia. Both in Rome and in Aricia she was especially, though not exclusively, a goddess of women. Even before her identification with the Greek divinity Artemis she had other functions, and after that identification the range of her activities was still further extended. The epithets applied to her show in how many fields she was believed to be active. She is called the goddess of childbirth (*Lucina* and *Ilithyia*), the guardian of mountains and woods (*custos montium et nemorum*), the queen of the woods (*regina nemorum*), the lover of streams (*laeta fluviis*), the huntress (*venatrix* and *iaculatrix*), the goddess of the moon (*lunata*), the glory of heaven (*decus caeli*), the goddess of night (*nocturna*), the queen of the skies (*regina polorum*), the virgin goddess (*virgo* and *innupta*), and the immaculate one (*casta*).

Some local epithets also, like those referring to her cult on the Aventine Hill (*Aventina*), on Mount Tifata near Capua (*Tifatina*), and at Ephesus (*Ephesia*),[1] are applied to her.

Of some of these numerous phases of the cult a few traces may still be found in the cult of the Madonna. For example, there are indications that the veneration of Diana as a virgin goddess has contributed something to the worship of the Virgin Mary. We know that one of the earliest churches erected in honor of Mary occupied the site of the famous temple of Diana at Ephesus. For although the original divinity of this sanctuary was an Asiatic goddess, she had been identified with the Greek Artemis and ultimately with the Roman Diana. Possibly the tradition[2] that Mary had once stayed in Ephesus was an element in the foundation of this church, which Cyril in one of his letters calls the Great Church (Ecclesia Magna). It was at Ephesus in 431 that the synod was held at which Mary was first designated Mother of God, and it is of some interest that the procession with which the populace celebrated the deification of Mary reproduced

[1] Cf. Carter in *Epitheta Deorum s. v. Diana.*

[2] A. Cuomo, *Saggio apologetico della bellezza celeste e divina di Maria S. S. Madre di Dio,* 209.

in such essentials as smoking censers and flaring torches the processions which for so many centuries had been an important part of the worship of Diana. Such processions have continued down to modern times on the occasion of the crowning of the Madonna in various parts of the world. The coronation of the Madonna at Pompeii in 1887 is an example.

But while the widespread worship of Diana as a virgin goddess undoubtedly facilitated the establishment of the cult of the Madonna and while there were direct contacts, such as that at Ephesus, between the pagan and the Christian ceremonies, we must guard against the danger of exaggerating the influence of any one ancient deity in the development of the cult of Mary. There were many virgin goddesses in the ancient religions besides Diana: among the Romans, Minerva (*virgo*), Bona Dea (like Mary called *sancta* and *sanctissima*); and among the Greeks, Artemis and Athene Parthenos. These too had helped to familiarize the world with the idea of a virgin goddess.

It is only in the same limited way that Diana's appellation of queen of heaven can be said to have influenced the designation of the Virgin Mary as queen or sovereign of the universe.[3] For other pagan divinities had contributed their quota to the establishment of this idea in the minds of the people. The Roman Juno had been called queen; the Greek Hera had borne the same title; the Carthaginians had their queen of heaven (Dea Caelestis); the Egyptian Isis, the Phoenician Astarte, and the Babylonian Mylitta had all been queens of heaven. The source of this appellative as applied to Mary is as multiplex as the title of immaculate virgin.

To the local epithets of Diana given above there are parallels in the case of the Madonna. For just as the ancients spoke of Diana of the Aventine or Diana of Tifata or Diana of Ephesus, modern churchmen speak of the Madonna of Monte Vergine, the Madonna of Pompeii, the Madonna of Einsiedeln, and many others. But here again the Madonna cult has been influenced not merely by Diana but by a practice that was common to many pagan cults and is illustrated by such examples as Juno of Argos, Juno of Lanuvium, and Venus of Cyprus, of Cythera, and of Mount Eryx.

The contention that the Feast of the Assump-

[3] Cf. St. Alfonso di Liguori, *Le glorie di Maria*, 8, 9, 11, 17, 21, 97, 198, 446 for such titles as Sovrana, Regina and Sovrana dell' Universo.

tion of the Blessed Virgin owes the date of its celebration to the festival of Diana seems to be without adequate support. There is, moreover, a discrepancy in date. The ancient festival took place on the thirteenth of August, while the modern feast is on the fifteenth.

XI. MINERVA AND THE
TEACHER'S PAY DAY

THE FESTIVAL of the nineteenth of March (Quinquạtrus), although it had originally been connected with the cult of Mars, came to be associated with Minerva and in historic times was regularly celebrated in her honor. Among other things she was a goddess of education and this day was of unusual importance in the school-year. Not only was it, like festal days in general, a holiday for pupils and teachers, but on it teachers received their stipend or honorarium (*minerval*). It was suggested by Hospinian,[1] a Swiss theologian of the sixteenth century, that a practice that obtained in some schools in his own time was a survival, with obvious modifications, of the ancient tradition. He tells us that it was the custom to call children to school with songs and to give them a present on this day that was sacred to Gregory the Great, the patron of scholars.

[1] Cf. Brand, *op. cit.*, I. 417 ff.

XII. THE GODDESS FORTUNA
AND GOOD OR BAD LUCK

THE FESTIVAL of Fortuna, "the goddess who brings" (*fero*), was held on the twenty-fourth of June. Difficult as is the question of the original significance of the cult, there is no doubt of an early connection with agriculture. We know that the farmers regarded Fortuna as a power who could bring them good crops or on the other hand manifest her displeasure by a lean year. Moreover, the time of year at which the festival took place and the nature of the festivities support the theory of an agricultural connection. It was the season of harvest and rustic celebrations were appropriate. Whether the fact that this was the time of the summer solstice was an element in determining the date of the festival is not certain, but in all probability it had something to do with it. The occasion was one of great merriment and the festival has sometimes been described as a summer Saturnalia.

The twenty-fourth of June is now St. John

the Baptist's Day, and the modern festival may owe its date to the pagan celebration. It is almost certain that it does if the summer solstice was a factor in the dating of the Roman holiday. Some even claim that the midsummer fires and other quaint customs till recently so common at this season in Great Britain and Ireland and on the Continent may be traced back to this festival. This contention, however, hardly admits of demonstration in detail. To be sure both the ancient and modern customs belong to the sphere of rustic merrymaking, and the practice of leaping over a fire cited by Brand[1] for various places in Great Britain has ancient Roman precedent. But neither of these facts bears directly on the question of actual influence of the ancient on the modern festival. For in the first place we have no evidence that the lighting of bon-fires was a part of the Roman festival; and secondly the leaping over a fire was a feature not of the festival of Fortuna on the twenty-fourth of June but of the feast of Pales (Parilia) on the twenty-first of April.

But the function of Fortuna was never in any period confined to agriculture. Even in the

[1] *Op. cit.*, I. 306 ff.

[99]

agricultural sphere her name, meaning as it does " the one who brings," connoted the idea of what we call fortune or luck. And this concept was equally apparent in another sphere in which her cult attained distinct importance, namely, that of women's lives and especially childbirth. Obviously there might be good or bad luck there. Indeed the cult showed its greatest development along this line of Fortune or Chance. We hear of the Fortune of the Imperial House, the Fortune of the Equestrian Order, the Fortune of the State, the Fortune that stays with one, the Fortune that deserts one, and so forth. Many other divinities in the Roman pantheon declined as the centuries passed but the history of the cult of Fortune shows constant expansion and steadily increasing vogue.

Of this goddess of Chance we have a survival in our frequent personification of fortune. Moreover, one of the emblems of the Roman goddess was a wheel, symbolizing mutability; and the " wheel of fortune " still survives in modern literature and life. It must be mentioned here, however, that according to one theory [2] the wheel that appears as an attribute

[2] Gaidoz, *Études de Myth. Gaul.*, I. 56 ff.

[100]

of Fortuna is not a symbol of mutability or in-
stability but a representation of the orb of the
sun. Under this interpretation Fortuna was a
solar divinity, and in support of this view much
emphasis is naturally laid on the occurrence
of the festival at the summer solstice. The
midsummer fires are pressed into service and
burn briskly in illustration of the theory. Attention is also drawn to the practice attested
for some places in England of rolling a wheel
down a hill on St. John the Baptist's Eve.[3]
Sometimes straw is twisted around the wheel
and lighted. This is held to symbolize the decline in the power of the sun as the days begin
to shorten. But plausible as some of the phases
of this explanation are, the evidence adduced
is not convincing.

There was another festival of Fortuna on
the first of April. This was the day on which
Roman women of the lower class honored Fortuna Virilis, who represented good fortune in
relations with men. As an important part of
the ceremonial of the day the women bathed in
the men's baths. In view of this fact it is not
surprising that on the introduction of the cult
of Venus Verticordia, a goddess of Greek and

[3] Brand, *op. cit.*, I. 298 ff.

ultimately Oriental origin, her festival (the Veneralia) was put on the same day. That the celebration involved a very considerable degree of license and foolery may be assumed. But there seems to be no evidence to support the suggestion that the practices of our April Fools' Day have their origin here. No satisfactory contact has ever been made between the customs now prevalent on the first of April and the rites either of Fortuna Virilis or of Venus Verticordia, who to large extent superseded her. Equally inconclusive is the theory of Barns,[4] who, partly on the basis of the affinity between Venus and the maiden-mother Arianrhod pointed out by Rhys in his *Hibbert Lectures,* thinks that All Fools' Day should be traced back to a Celtic form of this worship of Venus.

[4] *E. R. E.,* I. 332.

XIII. HERCULES AND THE OFFERING OF TITHES

IN THE offering of tithes by successful generals, traders and others at the Great Altar of Hercules in Rome on the twelfth of August, we possibly have a development of some simple offering of first-fruits made by the early Romans at a time when the community was chiefly agricultural. That it was the custom in various parts of ancient Italy to offer first-fruits to the gods we know. Sanctity still adheres to the first-fruits of the harvest in many countries of Europe, as Mannhardt and Frazer have shown. Such a custom as that which once obtained in some parts of Yorkshire, namely the cutting of the first grain by the vicar and its use in making the bread for communion, must be regarded as the relic of a religious idea that was widespread among the ancient peoples of Europe.

On the other hand it has never been finally demonstrated that the tithes offered to Hercules at the Great Altar were originally first-fruits of the harvest. All we can say is that they may have been offerings of this kind. According to some scholars the tithes were of Semitic origin, having been instituted in the cult of Hercules as a result of his identification with the Phoenician divinity Melcarth.[1]

Nor can we accept without many reservations the suggestion that the tithes of Hercules influenced the institution of tithes in the Christian Church. This system was adopted by the Christians from Semitic sources. They were familiar with it from their study of the Old Testament. At most, the tithes of Hercules could have influenced the Christian practice only in so far as they served to accustom the Romans to the system and thus paved the way for its establishment on the more comprehensive plan which the Christians adopted.

[1] Cf. Gardner in *The Journal of Hellenic Studies*, XIII, 75 (1892).

XIV. CASTOR AND POLLUX AND SOME MODERN SAINTS

THESE gods, generally called Dioscuri (sons of Zeus), although originally of Greek provenance, had been introduced into Rome from some Latin city, possibly Tusculum, and so were always considered by the Romans as of Italic origin. It was for this reason that their temple was built within the sacred boundary (*pomerium*) of the city.

Among other things Castor and Pollux were protectors of sailors. Both Greek and Roman ships often carried their images or used as their emblem the stars that so frequently appear in representations of the twin divinities.[1] This ancient emblem has not yet disappeared and may still be seen among the fisher-folk on the islands of the Mediterranean and along the coasts of southern Italy. Moreover, the electrical phenomenon that plays about the spars of ships on the Mediterranean after a storm was regarded of old as a manifestation of the gods'

[1] Cf. *Acts*, 28. 11.

presence.[2] This belief still survives in modified form. Modern sailors see in these lights indications of a divine presence but they attribute them to St. Elmo, a patron Saint of sailors. We do not, however, know very much about St. Elmo. Rendel Harris, pointing out that Romulus and Remus had attained some degree of sanctity among the Romans even before the introduction of Castor and Pollux, thinks that St. Elmo's name is connected with Remus, who is commemorated in San Remo on the coast of Italy, and indeed, so far as some of its forms are concerned, there is a resemblance.[3] But this theory is ingenious rather than convincing.

Professor Harris is also inclined to think that we have a reminiscence of Castor and Pollux in the pair of Saints Cosma and Damiano. Nor is he alone in this belief. Deubner,[4] though approaching the question from a different angle, has come to the same conclusion. The latter is of the opinion that the cult of these Saints, which flourished especially in Constantinople, inherited the tradition of Cas-

[2] Cf. Horace, *Od.*, I. 3. 2.
[3] Cf. *E. R. E.*, XII. 499.
[4] *De incubatione,* chap. IV.

tor and Pollux who, as he thinks, were worshipped as gods of healing in that city and in
whose temple the sick were accustomed to sleep
in hope of a cure (*incubatio*). That Cosma and
Damiano were medico-saints and that incubation was commonly practiced in their churches
in Constantinople is a well-established fact.[5]
And there can be little doubt that the same
custom obtained in their churches in other
places, for example in Rome, where they had
a famous sanctuary in the Forum. To be sure
the function of healing is not a feature of the
cult of the Dioscuri as we know it in most
places, but there are passages in ancient authors
which show that their temples were sometimes
used for incubation.[6]

[5] Hamilton, *Incubation*, 112.
[6] *Ibid.*, 120.

XV. AESCULAPIUS AND
INCUBATION

THE PRACTICE of incubation, referred to in the preceding section, was
chiefly associated with Aesculapius,
god of healing. He was a Greek divinity whose
cult was brought to Rome from Epidaurus in
293 B.C. An outbreak of plague was the immediate occasion of the introduction. The story
is that as the ship bearing the envoys who had
been sent to Epidaurus in regard to the establishment of the worship, sailed up the Tiber on
its return to Rome, the sacred snake which had
been brought from the Epidaurian temple
slipped overboard and swam to the island in
the Tiber. This was regarded as an indication
of the divine will and the temple of the god
was erected there. A few remains of it may
still be seen but they are not sufficient to enable
us to visualize it in detail.

While the Roman worship never attained
the fame of the cult at Epidaurus and other
places in Greece, it seems to have enjoyed a

moderate prosperity and in the second century of the Empire gained the favor of the emperor Antoninus Pius. Doubtless the system followed at the Roman sanctuary was the same as that at other temples of the god. The patients slept in the temple or in some other building equipped as a sleeping place within the precinct. Their belief was that the god would heal them while they slept or would tell them in a dream what they must do in order to be cured. While therapeutic treatment was applied in some cases, in the main it was a system of faith-cure, and innumerable successful cases were reported. Many inscriptions found at Epidaurus and elsewhere attest the gratitude of those who had regained their health through incubation.[1] It was, moreover, usual for the person cured to make a gift to the sanctuary. These offerings took different forms: an image of the part of the body that had been cured, or a statue or bas-relief or money. Ex-voto inscriptions also have been found at Rome and other places in the neighborhood. One inscribed on a marble stand discovered on the Tiber island records that it supported a silver image of a spleen that had been healed by the god.[2]

---

[1] Hamilton, *Incubation*, 17 ff.　　　[2] *Ibid.,* 67.

Incubation was adopted by the Church and has never ceased to be practiced. It was common in the early days of Christianity, flourished in the Middle Ages, and is still popular in some Catholic communities. That the cult of Aesculapius had more influence than any other in establishing the practice seems certain, but as has already been indicated, it was used in connection with other deities also. In the Christian churches it was Christ, instead of Aesculapius, who healed through the intercession of the Saints to whom the churches were dedicated. Hamilton [3] cites examples for the mediaeval period from Italy, Gaul, Germany, and Britain. The system was very similar to that of the pagans, and a vision that came to the patient as he slept in the church dedicated to some of the famous medico-saints was often the medium of the cure. Among the Saints venerated as physicians in the Middle Ages we hear of St. Martin at Tours, St. Julian at Arvernus, St. Maximinus at Trèves, and St. Peter and St. Paul at Cambridge.[4] Some of the maladies cured were paralysis, epilepsy, insanity, lameness, and blindness. The mediaeval Saints were as courageous in the face of serious dis-

[3] *Op. cit.*, 113, 114.   [4] *Ibid.*, 113.

eases as the priests of Aesculapius had ever
been. Among the churches where incubation is
still practiced may be mentioned the Cathedral
at Amalfi,[5] dedicated to St. Andrew, and chapels of St. John in Calabria and Sardinia, in
which incubation is especially common on St.
John's Eve. Trede [6] points to Santo Ciro of
Portici near Naples as the Aesculapius of that
town and its neighborhood. He was a physician
in his life time, and the power of healing has
been predicated of him ever since he became a
Saint. San Roque, the patron Saint of several
communities in Campania, is also thought to
continue those healing functions through which
in his life time he brought aid to so many of
those suffering from the plague.

As in the pagan Roman system, preliminary
rites always precede the sleeping in the sacred
edifice with a view to the establishment of the
proper attitude of mind on the part of the person seeking divine aid. That in both ancient
and modern times faith has proved salutary
and in some cases even resulted in cures is too
well-known to call for further demonstration.
In *Marius the Epicurean* [7] Pater speaks of the

<hr>

[5] Hamilton, *op. cit.*, 185 f.   [6] *Ibid.*, 203.
[7] Chap. III.

period of the Antonines, when the cult of Aesculapius was especially popular, as " an age of
valetudinarians." Without stopping to discuss
the historical accuracy of the phrase, it may
be admitted at least that such cults as those of
Aesculapius or of the healing Saints of mediaeval or modern times would be sure to make
a particularly strong appeal to valetudinarians
and hypochondriacs.

An interesting little item of medical history
has been pointed out in connection with the
temple of Aesculapius on the Tiber island.
When Christianity prevailed over paganism,
the sleeping porches of Aesculapius yielded to
the hospital of San Bartolomeo, which after so
many centuries still remains one of the hospi-
tals of Rome. But the therapeutic associations
of the place have gone even further. For it was
this Roman hospital of San Bartolomeo that
furnished inspiration and name for St. Bar-
tholomew's, the famous hospital in London.
Without a break the connection runs from the
Tiber island in the third century before Christ
to London in the twentieth century of the
Christian era.[8]

The usual attribute of Aesculapius was a

[8] Cf. Carter, *Religious Life of Ancient Rome,* 42.

staff with a serpent coiled around it. The suggestion that the staff symbolized the peripatetic function of the physician must be rejected as untenable insomuch as patients came to Aesculapius; he did not go to them. It is possibly of Oriental origin and its explanation may lie in the field of the magic wand. That the connection of the snake with healing is very ancient is as certain as the precise interpretation of the association is doubtful. Both staff and serpent have survived in the symbolistic devices of medical schools and societies all over the world. Error, however, sometimes creeps in, and the wand of Mercury, around which two snakes coil, is sometimes substituted for Aesculapius' staff with its single serpent. Medical organizations would be less favorable to the wand of Mercury as a symbol of their art if they bore in mind the fact that one of that god's functions was to conduct souls to the other world.

XVI. POSEIDON–NEPTUNE AND SAINT NICHOLAS

IT WAS only after his identification with the Greek god Poseidon that Neptune had any connection with the sea. That the identification had already been made by 399 B.C. is clear from his appearance in the *lectisternium* held at Rome in that year. There he is paired with Mercury and the combination obviously reflects ideas of over-seas trade. The cult came to Rome from southern Italy, where it was established in many places, the temples at Tarentum and Paestum being especially famous.

Some traces of this cult still remain. There is one in a statue of St. Anthony at Sorrento which shows a dolphin, a common attribute of the ancient sea-god Poseidon-Neptune. And it seems probable that in southern Italy, as in Greece,[1] St. Nicholas has to some extent taken the place of the pagan god. There is, for example, one feature of the festival held in honor

[1] Hyde, *Greek Religion and Its Survivals*, 62, 66.

of St. Nicholas at Bari on the Adriatic coast
that has all the appearance of a survival of the
Roman god. In a procession in which priests
and the general public participate boatmen and
fishermen carry the statue of the Saint down to
the seashore. There they place it on an elaborately decorated barge and take it out to sea.
Hundreds of boats follow in a sort of marine
triumphal procession.[2]

Moreover, in the command of the sea attributed to St. Nicholas in a devotional leaflet
of the Church,

*Santo Eroe, il quale col commando di sua voce
calmava i venti e le tempeste,*

there is a striking reminder of the picture of
Neptune given by Virgil: [3]

*Sic cunctus pelagi cecidit fragor, aequora postquam
Prospiciens genitor caeloque invectus aperto,
Flectit equos, curruque volans dat lora secundo.*

Trede is convinced that there are traces of
the Neptune cult in many other coast-towns of
southern Italy where St. Nicholas is especially
venerated. He even imagines that many of the

[2] Trede, *op. cit.*, II. 333.
[3] *Aeneid*, I. 154 ff:

[115]

statues or pictures of the Saint in the churches show the influence of the pagan representations of Poseidon and Neptune. But the evidence he furnishes is anything but convincing. It falls as far short of demonstrating his case as his argument that in the horse-breeding now carried on in the neighborhood of Paestum (called Poseidonia by the ancients) we have a survival of the pagan connection of Poseidon with horses and horse-racing.

XVII. THE MAN–GOD

LEGENDS of early Rome contain stories of the deification of mortals. Aeneas was said to have been deified and worshipped as Aeneas Indiges on the banks of the River Numicus. Romulus was reported to have been carried up to heaven from the Campus Martius. These were legends, but with the beginning of the Empire the deification of the ruler became an established part of the Roman system. Iulius Caesar was declared a god — Divus was the term used — by senatorial decree and his worship was put on a full ceremonial basis with temple, priests, and ritual. The same thing was done in the case of Augustus, Claudius, Vespasian, and Titus. This was one of the phases of Roman religion that showed extension and growth as the generations passed. For while only four of the first eleven emperors attained deification, from Nerva on almost all were made Divi. The last of the Divi was Romulus, son of Maxentius, who was deified in 307. The formal deification of a member of the imperial family never took place at Rome till after death. There is, however, plenty of evidence pointing to the worship of emperors in the provinces and in various parts of Italy during their life time.

Nor was deification confined to emperors or members of the imperial house. The poet Virgil attained after death a virtual deification, and apparently there were many who believed that Apollonius of Tyana had divine powers during his life time.

The surprising nature of this worship of mortals by the Romans fades out when we study their religious system as a whole, and recognize that in their minds no such chasm separated the human and the divine as modern theology has been prone to postulate. They believed in intermediate beings whose powers so far transcended those of ordinary men that they deserved to be classed with the gods. That so deep-seated a religious tradition as this was not likely to pass away is obvious; that it did not pass away we know from the evidence furnished by the cult of the Saints.

In this connection we must remember also the prevalence in the world at the beginning of our era of a belief in the coming of a deliverer.

This idea took different forms in different countries. To some persons Augustus was such a deliverer, as is seen from an inscription referring to his birthday.[1] With such an idea as this permeating the civilized world, men were more and more ready to recognize potentialities of divinity in men and to acclaim them as gods.

One phase of this cult of deified mortals has a very clear tradition, namely, the veneration of relics. Definite evidence of its existence among the Greeks is furnished by the oracle that emanated from Delphi that the Athenians should bring the bones of the hero Theseus to Athens. In Italy the bones of Virgil attained sanctity, and as the centuries passed they were regarded more and more as a guaranty of safety to the city of Naples where they were deposited. Furthermore, places associated with deified heroes were considered sacred, for example, the hut of Romulus preserved century after century on the Palatine Hill and the house of the Flavian family on the Quirinal Hill. We know also that Augustus regarded earth from a tomb as sacred.

[1] *Mitth. Arch. Inst. Ath.*, XXIV, 275 ff. (1899); Ramsay, *Letters to the Seven Churches,* 436; Iverach in *E. R. E.*, under Caesarism.

Reports of miracles wrought by human beings were common among the ancient Romans
and were accepted by the great mass of the
people without question. The Emperor Vespasian was believed to have the power of healing; Apollonius of Tyana was credited with
miracles; and many other examples might be
cited. How prevalent the belief was in the second century is indicated by Lucian's [2] ridicule
of it.

Roman society, therefore, at the time when
Christianity emerged, was wholly familiar with
the ideas of a man-god, the sacrosanct quality
of relics, and the frequent occurrence of miracles. The Christians adapted themselves to
the pagan attitude. They matched the miracle-
workers of the pagans with wonder-working
Saints; and with their success the number of
miracles increased. The sanctity of relics, well-
established as it had been among the pagans,
acquired far greater vogue in Christian times
and was given a degree of emphasis that it had
never had before. The idea showed extension
also in the division of the remains of a Saint and
in the efficacy attached even to the smallest
relic. Moreover, we find the term Divus which

[2] *De dea Syria.*

[120]

had acquired its special connotation through the deification of emperors applied to Christian Saints. Examples are Divus Ianuarius (S. Gennaro), Divus Iosephus (S. Giuseppe), and Diva Agatha (S. Agatha). And at the end of this word's long history is its faded application in modern times to actresses and opera-singers.

Like the deified heroes and emperors of pagan times the Saints were honored with altars, sacred edifices, incense, lights, hymns, ex-voto offerings, festivals with illuminations and high hilarity, prayers and invocations. They became intermediate divinities with intercessional and tutelary powers.

That St. Paul and Jesus himself would have regarded many of these beliefs and practices as wholly foreign to the spirit of Christianity is certain. Some of the early Christians themselves protested against the cult of the Saints: for example, Vigilantius and Faustus in the fifth century. But on the other side were such great apologists as Augustine, Jerome, Ambrose, Chrysostom, and Basil, who though claiming that God alone was worshipped, expressed full belief in the efficacy of the intercession of the Saints.

XVIII. THE MOTHER OF THE
GODS AND THE BAPTISM
OF BLOOD

THE CULT of this Phrygian divinity, variously called the Mother of the Gods, Cybele, the Great Mother or the Idaean Mother, was introduced into Rome in 204 B.C. Doubt, discouragement, and fear in regard to the issue of the war with Hannibal, who was still in Italy with his army of invasion, drove the Romans to seek the aid of foreign gods. A commission was sent to the East, the sacred stone, the symbol of the goddess, was brought to Rome and the cult was established on the Palatine Hill. It was the first Oriental cult introduced into Rome.

The goddess was a nature divinity, mother of gods, and mighty mistress of all forms of life. With her was associated Attis, whose death symbolized the dying of vegetation and his resurrection its revival in the spring. What part Attis had in the Roman cult of the Mother in republican times is not clear, but during the empire, especially from the time of the monuments and inscriptions pertaining to the *taurobolium*, the references to him are numerous. He is one of the redeemer-gods of pagan religion.

Although this cult was one of the last to yield to Christianity and persisted obstinately after most of the other pagan forms of worship had passed away, it left but few traces of its protracted dominance. To be sure points of contact with the Virgin Mary have been pointed out. One of Mary's titles, " the Mother of God " (Gran Madre di Dio), has inevitable reminiscences of the pagan " Mother of the Gods." Moreover, many a visitor to Rome and student of sculpture has commented on the resemblance between the statues of the two. Furthermore, we know that the shrine of the Virgin on Monte Vergine near Avellino in the Apennines not far from Naples, which is visited each year by thousands of pilgrims, attracted by the fame of the wonder-working image there, was once the site of a temple of the Great Mother. That they were confused in people's minds is shown by the question which an unbeliever addressed to Abbot Isidore of Pelusium in the sixth century. He asked what the difference was between the Magna

Mater of the pagans and the Magna Mater
Maria of the Christians. But mother-god-
desses, whatever their origin or special characteristics, are bound to have certain features
in common. Nor is there much reason for sur-
prise in finding in Claudia's prayer [1] to the
Great Mother a tone analogous to that of any
prayer to the sanctissima Maria in modern
times: "Hear my prayer, thou who art the
gentle mother of the gods."

During the days of the Megalesia, the festival celebrated in honor of the Great Mother
on the fourth and the tenth of April, her priests
collected money from the people. We cannot,
however, see in this the origin of the institution
of begging friars. There were mendicant
Orphic priests as early as the time of Plato,
and in all probability other cults had a similar
system. All that can be said in regard to the
influence of the begging priests of Cybele is that
they were among those who contributed to the
establishment of the practice.

In regard to the relation of the *taurobolium*
to Christianity no satisfactory results have ever
been reached. The rite was among the most
striking and curious of all those pertaining to

[1] Ovid, *Fasti,* IV. 319.

the cult of the goddess. The devotee passed into a crypt the top of which consisted of boards widely spaced or of a metal grill, and down upon him rained the blood of a bull sacrificed above. It was literally a baptism of blood. It cleansed the sins away. The person who submitted to it was " born again." Some ancient records speak of its efficacy as limited to twenty years; according to others it lasted forever. Everyone will observe the parallelism with the Christian doctrine of rebirth to righteousness. But apparently it is only a case of parallelism. It is a manifestation in two contemporary religions of an idea that was then filtering through the Mediterranean world. There is certainly no evidence that the Christians derived it from the cult of the Great Mother. The earliest known taurobolic inscription is dated A.D. 133, but Paul had preached the doctrine that men must be born again long before.

XIX. THE EGYPTIAN DEITIES:
ISIS, SERAPIS, AND
HARPOCRATES (HORUS)

IT WAS the Hellenized cult of Isis as organized by Ptolemy the First that the Romans knew. While retaining some of the characteristics of the Isis of the older Egyptian religion, she had, through the Ptolemaic reorganization or in the process of syncretism, acquired other functions. She was goddess of heaven, of earth, of the sea, and of the world below. The syncretism that made her in the eyes of her devotees the supreme arbitress of man's lot in life and resulted in her worship as Isis-Fortuna, manifested itself with still wider comprehensiveness in the cult of Isis Panthea, in which she seemed to have absorbed the functions of all other divinities.

With Isis in the Ptolemaic form of the cult were associated Serapis and Harpocrates. The origin of the former has been the subject of long and divergent discussion. Apparently his

cult was introduced by Ptolemy the First and
it may have been brought to Alexandria from
Sinope. While the identification with Osiris,
who in earlier Egyptian belief was the husband
of Isis, explains some phases of the worship
of Serapis, there are other aspects of his cult
that show distinct Hellenistic influence. Like
Isis he had wide and various functions. Among
other things he appears as a sun-god.

Harpocrates, a phase of the old Egyptian
Horus, was the son of Isis. He too had contacts with solar worship and was adored as the
newly-risen sun.

There is evidence that the cult of Isis and
her associates spread from Alexandria to the
island of Delos. And from there it may have
been taken to the Campanian port Puteoli, as
there was a brisk trade between the two places.
Its existence in Puteoli in the second century
before Christ is well attested.[1] It may have
come to Rome from Campania or it may have
reached the city more directly. There is a
strong probability that the tradition which as-
cribes its introduction to the time of Sulla is
correct. At any rate we know that it was suf-

[1] *C. I. L.*, X. 1781; Dubois, *Mélanges d'archéologie
et d'histoire*, XXII, 47 ff. (1902).

ficiently strong by the year 58 B.C. to cause some alarm among the Roman authorities, for the altars of Isis on the Capitoline Hill were destroyed at that time by order of the Senate. Persecution, however, seems to have had the usual result of defeating its own purpose. In the first century of the Empire, probably in Caligula's reign,[2] Isis and Serapis were recognized as state gods. From that time on their worship flourished. It was in a temple of Isis and Serapis in the Campus Martius that Vespasian and Titus passed the night before they made their triumphal entry into Rome in 71. In the second and third centuries the cult was one of the chief rivals of Christianity. There were as many as seven temples of the cult in Rome at this time.[3]

Many features of this Egyptian cult were absorbed by the Christian Church and still survive:

1. THE IDEA OF A DIVINE TRINITY

To mention first a fundamental point of theology, it is probable that the worship of the Egyptian triad Isis, Serapis, and the child Horus

[2] Wissowa, op. cit., 354.
[3] Legge, Forerunners and Rivals of Christianity, I. 79.

helped to familiarize the ancients with the idea of a triune god and was not without influence in the formulation of the doctrine of the trinity as set forth in the Nicaean and Athanasian creeds.[4] One cannot of course be sure that the doctrine of trinity emerged first in Egypt. In Indian religion there is the trinity of Brahmā, Śiva, and Visnu, and this may be of very early origin. But it was not only the religious thinkers of the Orient who had been attracted by the concept of trinity. The Neoplatonists had elaborated trinitarian theories, and in the writings of Plotinus, who was doubtless influenced by Plato's *Timaeus,* the Supreme Reality appears in the trinitarian form of the Good, the Intelligence, and the World-Soul.[5] That Neoplatonism was one of the operative factors in the development of Christian theology seems certain.

2. Isis, Mother of Horus, and the Madonna and Child

Further, the idea of Isis as the mother of the child Horus was in many minds transferred to Mary, mother of God. " Remember," said

---

[4] Legge, *op. cit.,* I. 88 f.
[5] Fulton in *E. R. E.,* XII. 458.

Gregory the Great, when issuing his instructions to a missionary to the Saxon heathens, " that you must not interfere with any traditional belief or religious observance that can be harmonized with Christianity." And the policy of the Church toward the Saxons was not unique. The same method was used in dealing with pagans everywhere. It was the bridge over which untold thousands passed from paganism to the new faith. Without this adaptability Christianity might not have succeeded. The shift from Isis to Mary was one of the easiest and most obvious. There are extant statuettes and figurines of Isis nursing Horus which are marked by a striking similarity to familiar representations of the Madonna and Child. It is said that sometimes images of this kind have been mistaken for representations of Mary and Jesus and have actually been worshipped in Christian Churches.[6] Nor is it only as the infant son of Isis that Horus has been confused with Jesus. On the wall of a crypt in Alexandria there is a painting in which a youthful Christ of the beardless type is represented as treading on serpents and trampling on a lion and a crocodile. This is said to

---

[6] Drexler in Roscher's *Lexikon*, II. 431.

go back to a well-known representation of Horus.[7]

3. IMAGES OF ISIS AND OF THE MADONNA

MOREOVER, in the bedizened images of the Madonna in many Churches in southern Italy and elsewhere one cannot but see a repetition of the extravagant ornamentation that characterized some of the statues of Isis, such as the figure of the goddess described in an inscription [8] in Spain, with its emeralds, pearls, and other jewels.

An interesting religious tradition lies in the statement of Mackenzie Wallace [9] that an image of the Madonna, of especial sanctity, was from time to time taken by rich residents of Moscow to their houses. Its presence there was believed to bring a blessing on the family. This practice is one of great antiquity, for we know that the image of Isis was sometimes taken to the house of a devotee and left there for a brief period. Whether the modern practice is derived directly from the ancient is difficult to say. The evidence is hardly conclu-

[7] *Ibid.*, where other examples are given.
[8] *C. I. L.*, II. 3386.
[9] *Russia*, 353.

sive. But at least we have in the practice as
it exists in the Madonna cult the survival of a
belief that was well established in ancient times.
Nor is the custom confined to the Madonna.
The holy Bambino of the Church of the Ara
Coeli on the Capitoline Hill in Rome has sometimes been borrowed from the Church and
taken to private homes.

4. CULT-EPITHETS OF ISIS AND THE MADONNA

THE similarity between the cult-epithets of Isis
and those of the Virgin Mary has often been
pointed out.[10] While many of the parallels
claimed, especially in the list given by Beauregard,[11] are imaginary, others are undoubtedly
valid and furnish us with additional evidence
of the contact of the two cults. Correspond-
ing to Isis Regina are familiar appellations of
the Virgin: Sovrana, Sovrana dell' Universo,
Regina. To Isis Mater corresponds the Christian Mater Domini; to Isis Furva the Madonna
Addolorata, to Isis Pelagia the Regina Maris
(Madonna del Porto Salvo), to Dea Potens [12]

[10] Hampson, *Medii aevi kalendarium*, 16–17, 145–146.
[11] *Les divinités égyptiennes*, 174, 175, 341.
[12] Apuleius, *Met.*, XI. 1, 16, 22.

Maria della Potenza, to Isis Soteira [13] Madonna
del Ajuto.

5. ISIS, HORUS, AND SAINTS

SOME legends of saints have also been attributed to the influence of the Isis cult. Usener [14]
sees traces of Isis Pelagia in the legends of St.
Pelagia; others see the influence of the Egyptian divinities in the stories of St. Onuphrius
and St. Catherine. But the arguments advanced are not convincing. A more plausible
case is made for the influence of the Horus cult
on the legend of St. George. For some monuments show Horus as a young man, on horse-
back, killing a crocodile with a spear, and it
may easily be that this representation has influenced the familiar group of St. George and
the dragon.[15] Still another theory seeks to es-
tablish a connection between Horus and St.
Michael.

6. THE ELEVATION OF SACRED OBJECTS

BUT there are still other features of the cult of
Isis that have left their impression on modern

[13] Cf. Apuleius, *ibid.*, XI. 25, humani generis sospita-
trix. Beauregard, *op. cit.*, 341, compares the appellation
Notre Dame de Bon-Secours.

[14] *Die Legende der h. Pelagia,* Bonn, 1879.

[15] E. Meyer, in Roscher's *Lexikon,* I. 2748.

religious rites. Among the wall-paintings uncovered at Herculaneum there is one which
shows a priest of Isis on the portico of a temple
holding up a vase, presumably containing the
holy water of the Nile, for the adoration of
the devotees in the precinct below.[16] Obviously this is an example of the gesture of ele-
vating sacred objects, the continuance of which
is seen in the Catholic ceremony of the mass.

7. MONACHISM, PAGAN AND CHRISTIAN

IT IS probable also that the organization of the
Christian clergy was influenced by the system
that obtained in the cult of Isis. That the
priestly service of the Church should show signs
of its contacts with the other religions in the
midst of which it grew up was, in view of its
policy of adaptation, inevitable; and a study
of all the priestly systems in vogue during the
second and third centuries indicates that it is
in the elaborate and specialized service of Isis
that we must look for the prototype of the
Christian clerical body rather than in any of
the sacerdotal groups connected either with
other Oriental cults in Rome or deities imported from Greece or indigenous cults of Italy.

[16] Mau-Kelsey, *Pompeii. Its Life and Art,* 177, 178.

But perhaps the most important phase of Isiac influence in the field of service and personnel is to be found in that monachism which we know to have been part of the worship of Isis and which has from the fourth century been so significant an element in the organization of the Catholic Church. This is an old and vexed question. Many scholars have denied any influence of the recluses of Isis and Serapis on Christian monachism. They have suggested other theories of its origin, variously attributing it to Neoplatonism or the practices of the Druids or Orphism or Buddhist asceticism or Jewish monasticism with special reference to the Essenes. And there are some writers who refuse to admit the possibility of any outside influence. For example, Cabrol [17] says that "Christian monasticism is a plant that has grown up on Christian soil, nourished exclusively on principles of Christianity." So sweeping a statement will carry conviction to no one who has studied the question. Only those will accept it whose habit is to bury their heads in the dry sands of unthinking credulity.

The explanation of the question does not really involve any special difficulty. From the

[17] *E. R. E.*, VIII. 783.

data industriously collected by so many generations of scholars it is clear that asceticism was a traditional feature of many ancient cults. Originating in an intense desire for closer communion of the spirit with God — a common and natural religious attitude — it became established under various forms in different communities, and in the early days of Christianity was part of the religious conditions of the period. The verses in the New Testament to which the advocates of an independent origin for Christian monachism always appeal are in no sense an indication of independent thinking on the part of the Christian brotherhood. They are merely a sign of the times.

But apart from the inheritance of a common religious practice the evidence seems to point to something more specific. For while it seems likely that influence should be attributed to the Essenes as well as to the teaching of the Orphists and Neoplatonists, the most direct source lies in the recluses connected with the cult of Isis and Serapis.[18] Of the existence of these we have known for a long time. The

[18] Weingarten, *Der Ursprung des Mönchtums im nach-constantinischen Zeitalter*. Cf. Bouché-Leclerq in his article " Les reclus du Serapeum de Memphis," *Mélanges Perrot*, 1903, 17.

fragments of papyrus containing records of the
hermits of the Serapeum in Memphis were
found as far back as 1820. These fragments
make it clear that anchorites devoted to the
worship of the Egyptian divinities lived there.
Some of them took part in the services, while
others seemed to have lived in the strictest se-
clusion. Kenyon [19] dates the papyrus in the
second century before Christ. Doubtless there
were similar monastic groups in other centers
of the Egyptian cult. That there were devotees of this kind in Alexandria is known.
And Legge [20] has reason for giving credence
to the story that when the Serapeum was
destroyed toward the end of the fourth century after Christ and the Alexandrian religion
perished after a notably successful career of
seven centuries, many of the devotees transferred their allegiance to the Christian faith.
Moreover St. Anthony, who is often spoken of
as the father of Christian monasticism, was a
hermit in Egypt, and in its early days monasticism both in Italy and other parts of the Western Empire showed the influence of the An-
tonian system. Nor can the influence of St.

[19] *The Palaeography of Greek Papyri*, 4, 38.
[20] *Op. cit.*, I. 84.

Pachomius, who established the first monastery (*cenobium*) about A.D. 320, near Dendera in southern Egypt, be disregarded in the history of Christian monasticism.

8. OTHER ISIAC SURVIVALS

OTHER points of survival or resemblance should be noted briefly. A characteristic feature of the service of Isis was the use of the bronze rattle called *sistrum*. This may be the source of the practice of tinkling a bell in certain ceremonies of the Catholic Church. An instrument of the ancient form is said to be still in use in religious ceremonies in Abyssinia.[21] Further, the shaven heads of the initiates of Isis are said to be the ultimate source of the tonsure in the Catholic priesthood.[22] Moreover, the veiling of women in Isiac ceremonies has been suggested as the origin of the custom of women's heads being covered in church.[23] There may be influence in both these cases, but it should be pointed out that so far as the tonsure is concerned the tradition is somewhat precarious. As a matter of fact the tonsure did not become

[21] Roscher, *Lexikon*, II. 429.
[22] Bury, in Gibbon, *Decline and Fall of the Roman Empire*, IV, App. 3, 527.
[23] Legge, *op. cit.*, I. 86.

a matter of ecclesiastical ordinance till the seventh century. There is more continuity of practice in the use of the white linen robe as an article of sacerdotal costume. Worn by the priests of Isis, it is still an essential part of ecclesiastical dress. Again, there is a striking survival in the field of ex-voto offerings. Isis, among her numerous functions, was a goddess of health, and it was the custom of those who believed that they had been healed by her divine favor to hang up in her temple a sculptured or painted representation of the part of the body that had been affected. " Help me, O Goddess, for the many painted tablets in thy temples show that thou hast healing power." So wrote Tibullus [24] of Isis. And Juvenal's [25] line that Isis provided a living for painters doubtless refers to the same thing. The offerings made by devout Catholics after recovery from illness and displayed in churches constitute a direct continuation of the ancient practice. Finally, the Isiac processions had many features that cannot but impress the student of religious survivals: the carrying of sacred images, the elaborately decorated places where

[24] I. 3. 27–28.
[25] XII. 28: Pictores quis nescit ab Iside pasci?

the procession paused, the burning of incense, the marching of the white-clad priests, and the whole-souled devotion of the initiates as they invoked the favor of their goddess, who could give them happiness in both this world and the next. The scene has undeniable points of similarity to the religious processions in Catholic cities of Europe. Well might the Emperor Hadrian,[26] writing from Alexandria in A.D. 124, say that it was difficult to distinguish between the Christians and the devotees of Serapis.

[26] The letter is to the consul Servianus: Illic (i.e., in Alexandria) qui Serapem colunt Christiani sunt, et devoti sunt Serapi qui se Christi episcopos dicunt (*Historia Augusta,* Saturninus. Teubner edition, Hohl, II. 227).

XX. ADONIS AND THE CRADLE OF JESUS

THE CULT of Adonis was known to the Romans at least as early as the Augustan age, as is shown by Ovid's reference,[1] and there are a number of allusions to it in the later imperial period. The Hellenized form in which it reached Rome seems to indicate that it was introduced from some Greek site rather than from Byblos in Phoenicia where it originated. Of it we have in all probability a survival in the worship of the cradle of Christ in Catholic Churches on Christmas Eve. For the rite as celebrated in such churches as S. Maria Maggiore in Rome goes back to the adoration of the cave in Bethlehem where Christ was born. The institution of the practice there is as early as the time of Constantine, and we have Origen's testimony that almost any one in Bethlehem could point out the scene of the birth. But this cave had had earlier religious associations. It was the place where

[1] *Ars Amatoria,* I. 75.

the youthful Adonis, beloved of Aphrodite, who died before his time, was bewailed by his devotees.[2]   Helena, the mother of Constantine, rescued it from the heathen and built a basilica there, to which Constantine himself added rich equipment.

[2] See Usener, *Weihnachtsfest,* 283.

XXI. MITHRAS, PERSIAN GOD
OF LIGHT

WHILE Mithras, a Persian god of light, was known to some Romans at an earlier date,[1] his cult does not seem to have been introduced into Rome till about the end of the first century of the Empire. Nor is there any evidence that it made much headway in the first period of its establishment. The earliest sanctuaries that can be dated with any degree of certainty belong to the reigns of Trajan and Hadrian. The favor of the Emperor Commodus, who is said to have been initiated into the mysteries of the cult, gave it prestige, and from that time its popularity steadily increased. From the inscriptions we see that not only the poor and lowly were numbered among the adherents of the god but also persons of noble birth and exalted social or official position. By the Emperors Diocletian and Maximian Mithras was designated "patron of their Empire" (*fautor imperii*

[1] Plutarch, *Pomp.*, 24.

sui). The cult attained its greatest popularity in the second and third centuries. It did not pass away till the fourth.

Our records of the cult — chiefly sculptured monuments and inscriptions — show a certain amount of confusion. For example, on more than one monument Mithras is seen with the Sun-god, either seated at a table with him and others, or riding in his chariot with him, or associated with him in some other way. On the other hand many inscriptions identify Mithras with the Sun-god, dedications being found " To the Invincible Sun Mithras." In view of these facts we must infer that while the sculptured monuments found in such profusion throughout the western part of the Empire include the representation of beliefs or legends of Persian or Babylonian origin, in the minds of many Roman devotees Mithras was identical with the Sun-god.

There are numerous indications of contacts and mutual influence between Mithraism and Christianity. Of their similarity we have evidence in St. Augustine's [2] statement that Mith-

[2] *Johann. Evang. Tract.*, VII. But Cumont, *T. et M.*, II. 59, pointing out that Mithras is not mentioned by name, contends that the words used, *iste pileatus*, " the one in the cap," refer to Attis rather than to Mithras.

[144]

raists used to say that their god was a Christian too.

1. Legends of the Birth of Mithras and of Jesus

IT HAS been suggested [3] that the gospel story of the birth of Jesus and the adoration of the Magi [4] contains elements derived from the Mithras legend. More concretely and effectively Cumont [5] draws attention to the parallel furnished by those sculptured monuments which show shepherds watching the miraculous birth of Mithras from the rock to the story of the adoration of the shepherds at the birth of Christ.[6]

2. Mithras and the Ascension Story

ANOTHER Mithraic relief shows Mithras ascending to heaven in the chariot of the Sun-god, and comparison has often been made with the ascension of Elijah. Points of contact with the account of Christ's ascension have also been claimed. At any rate it is clear that both cults stressed an ascension story.

[3] Jean Reville in *Études publiées en hommage à la faculté de théologie de Montauban*, 1901, 339 f.

[4] Matthew, 2. 1 ff.

[5] Cf. Legge, *op. cit.*, II. 242.

[6] Luke, 2. 8 ff.

3. Baptism, Confirmation, and Communion

But there are still more striking resemblances. The Mithraists prescribed baptism for their initiates, seeing in immersion a means of expiating sin.[7] They had also a confirmation, which conferred the power of combating evil demons. And — perhaps the most notable resemblance of all — they had a communion. Certainly this is the most plausible explanation of that scene on the sculptured monuments where Mithras, the Sun-god, and initiates of Mithras are shown at a table, eating and drinking. It was these resemblances that drove Justin Martyr [8] to exclaim that Mithraism was a diabolical imitation of Christianity. But it is not always clear which is the borrower.

4. "Brothers" and "Fathers" among the Mithraists

The practice of calling one another "brother" and designating their priest as "father" may easily have passed from the Mithraists to the Christians.

[7] Porphyry, *De antro nymph.*, 18; Tertullian, *De praescrip.*, 40.

[8] *First Apology*, 56.

[146]

5. MITHRAISM AND THE DIVINE RIGHT OF KINGS

ONE of the tenets of Mithraism was the divinity of kings, though it is not possible for us to determine whether this doctrine was the cause or the effect of the favor which the cult found with the kings of Persia and other Asiatic countries. The influence of this belief was profound and long-enduring. It undoubtedly tended to develop that attitude of mind, so common among Asiatics, that insisted on seeing in rulers and other men of high station indications of divinity which merited ceremonial veneration during their life time and formal deification after death. We have the record of Roman generals in Asia who were honored with sacred rites, and these were merely forerunners of the long list of deified emperors of Rome. But while this idea of deified mortals found its most notable exemplification in the Divi, it did not pass away when the cult of the emperors perished. It lingered long in dynastic theories of Western Europe. It survives in such phrases as " sacred majesty " and " divine right of kings."

6. MITHRAISM AND RITES OF THE GYPSIES

AN interesting suggestion has been made that traces of Mithraism may be found in the religious ceremonies of some tribes of Gypsies.[9] A specific example is cited from the practices of the Gypsies who pay such special attention to the veneration of St. Sara in the Île de la Camargue, Bouches du Rhône. It is claimed that just as the shrine of St. Sara rests upon an ancient altar dedicated to Mithras, so the worship of the Saint still retains elements of the Mithraic cult upon which it has been superimposed. The Gypsies of this neighborhood are supposed to be the descendants of the ancient Iberians, who are known to have been acquainted with Mithraism.

7. MITHRAIC ORIGIN OF SUNDAY

OUR observance of Sunday as the Lord's Day is apparently derived from Mithraism. The argument that has sometimes been used against this claim, namely that Sunday was chosen because the resurrection occurred on that day, is not well supported. As a matter of fact the

[9] *E. R. E.*, VI. 464. Cf. *Journal of Gypsy Lore Society*, N. S., I, 92–95 (1907) and I, 391 (1908). Cf. also Winstedt, *ibid.*, II, 338 ff. (1909).

first Christians adhered to the Jewish practice of keeping Saturday. Apparently the observance of Sunday began with the Pauline Churches in Asia Minor, where the Mithraists, numerous and influential, had celebrated Sunday long before the Christian era. For even in those forms of Mithraism that did not identify Mithras with the Sun-god, the latter was always prominent in the cult. An interesting and significant phrase occurs in the Didache, " on the Lord's Day of the Lord," [10] which shows that there was another Lord's Day besides that of the Christians. This could have been none other than the Mithraists' day of their Lord, the Sun. On that day there were special Mithraic services and prayers. And when they prayed, the Mithraists like other sun-worshippers, faced the east in the morning, the south at noon, and the west at sun-set. Nor has this practice entirely passed away. There is a survival of it in the custom still followed in Catholic and some Episcopalian Churches of facing east during certain prayers.

[10] *E. R. E.,* under " Sunday."

XXII. OTHER SUN–GODS

ONE OF the dominant religious ideas of the second and third centuries was the belief in the divinity of the Sun. We have already seen the elements of solar worship involved in the cults of Attis, Serapis, Adonis, and Mithras. But there were other important sun-cults also. The Emperor Elagabalus introduced into Rome the worship of the Syrian sun-god Elagabal, whose priest he had been in the East and for whom he was named. And in the year 274 the Emperor Aurelian dedicated a magnificent temple in Rome to " the Unconquerable Sun-god " (Deus Sol Invictus), who probably was the chief divinity of Palmyra in Syria.

1. THE SUN-GOD OF AURELIAN AND CHRISTMAS

THIS divinity is of especial interest for our inquiry, for his annual festival fell on the twenty-fifth of December and its relation to Christmas

has been a matter of protracted discussion.[1]
Obviously the season of the winter solstice,
when the strength of the sun begins to increase,
is appropriate for the celebration of the festival
of a sun-god. The day in a sense marks the
birth of a new sun. But the reason for its being chosen as the day for the commemoration
of Christ's nativity is not so evident. According to some scholars the time of year of the
birth of Christ most widely accepted in the
earlier period in the West was the end of March.
The author of the pseudo-Cyprianic treatise
De pascha computus, which was written in 243,
gives the twenty-eighth of March as the date.
He states that Sunday, the twenty-fifth of
March, the vernal equinox, was the first day
of creation; and that the sun and moon were
created on Wednesday the twenty-eighth.
Then after a highly fanciful series of computa-
tions he arrives at the conclusion that Christ
was born on the same day of the year as that
on which the sun was created. Apparently
others in this early period thought that the
twenty-fifth of March was the date. But this
discrepancy of a few days is not important.

[1] Duchesne, *Christian Worship,* 261 ff.; Kirsopp Lake
in *E. R. E.,* III. 601 ff.

Subsequently, it has been claimed, the date of the birth was shifted from the twenty-eighth or twenty-fifth of March to the twenty-fifth of December as a result of the belief that while the March date marked the conception — in a sense the beginning of the Incarnation — of Jesus, the birth took place nine months later. On the basis of this argument the fact that the date of Christ's birth falls on the same day as the festival of " the Unconquerable Sun " is said to be an accident. But this is hardly a satisfactory explanation. The identity of date is more than a coincidence. To be sure the Church did not merely appropriate the festival of the popular sun-god. It was through a parallelism between Christ and the sun that the twenty-fifth of December came to be the date of the nativity. That an equation between the two had been instituted at a period earlier than any celebration of the nativity we know from the *De pascha computus* referred to above. Indeed the most significant element in that document is just this parallelism. Once the equation had been made, the appropriateness of selecting for the commemoration of the nativity that day on which the power of the sun began to increase was obvious enough.

Even Epiphanius,[2] the fourth century metro-
politan of Cyprus, though giving the sixth of
January as the date of birth, connects the event
with the solstice. Moreover, the diversion of
the significance of a popular pagan holiday was
wholly in accord with the policy of the Church.
Of the actual celebration of a festival of the
nativity, it should be added, there is no satisfactory evidence earlier than the fourth century. Its first observance in Rome on December the twenty-fifth took place in 353 or
354 (Usener) or in 336 (Duchesne). In Constantinople it seems to have been introduced in
377 or 378.

2. Sun-Worship and St. Elias

Another trace of ancient sun-worship may
possibly be found in southern Italy in the cult
of St. Elias. Those who favor this theory point
to the wheel which appears in some representations of the Saint. They see in it an inheritance
from the chariot of the Greek sun-god Helius.

[2] *Haer.* LI. 22. 3–11 (ed. Holl): "The birth of our
Lord Jesus Christ, or the perfect incarnation, which is
called Epiphany, took place thirteen days after the beginning of the increase of light. For it was necessary that
this also be a type of the number of our Lord Jesus Christ
himself and of his twelve apostles, which filled up the
number of the thirteen days of the increase of the light."

There may be something in this contention. There is, moreover, some degree of similarity in the names Elias and Helius. On the whole, however, it seems likely that any connection with Helius that may be found here is distinctly subordinate to the influence of the story of the Hebrew prophet Elijah whose chariot of fire furnishes quite as satisfactory a prototype for the symbolism of St. Elias as the chariot of the sun-god.[3]

[3] See Hyde's discussion of St. Elias and Helius in *Greek Religion and Its Survivals*, 78–80.

XXIII. PRAYER AND ADORATION

AS A RULE the ancient Romans stood while praying, as we know from many passages in Latin authors. And while there is evidence to show that kneeling was an old Italic practice, it seems probable that in historic times worshippers knelt only when the occasion was one of such urgency as to call for a special demonstration of humility and self-abandonment. It is also undoubtedly true that the increase in the influence of the cults imported from Greece and the Orient tended to make the practice more common. In the ceremony of the *supplicatio*, for example, a rite of Greek origin, the women knelt before the statues of the gods. We hear also of cases where worshippers beat their heads against the door-posts of temples, or wholly prostrated themselves, sweeping altars or the floor of temples with their hair.

During his enunciation of the prayer it was usual for the worshipper to raise his hands to heaven, and there are sepulchral inscriptions containing reliefs that show raised hands and open palms. On some occasions, however, the procedure was different and it was essential that the one praying should touch the altar with his hands. This contact with the sacred object was believed to intensify the coercive efficacy of the prayer upon the god.

The Romans said grace before dinner; [1] and there was at least a silent grace when after the dinner proper, before the dessert was served, parts of the food were offered to the household gods. Before the banquet at Anchises' tomb Aeneas made libations and addressed his father's spirit. [2]

Closely connected with prayer in the minds of the Romans was adoration (*adoratio*). This was sometimes a preliminary to prayer but was practiced on many occasions when no prayers were said. It consisted in placing the right hand upon the mouth (*ad ora*) as one stood before or passed by a temple or altar or statue. In ancient times indeed to throw a kiss to a deity was a sufficiently solemn bit of ceremonial practice. Nor was the kiss always thrown.

[1] Quint., *Decl.*, 301, p. 187, Ritter: Invitavi ad cenam . . . venisti . . . et adisti mensam, ad quam cum venire coepimus, deos invocamus.

[2] *Aeneid*, V. 77 ff.

Cicero tells us of a statue of Hercules at Agrigentum whose mouth and chin were worn away by the kisses of devotees.[3] A passage in Lucretius[4] probably refers to something similar. The practice was not of course distinctively Roman. The Greeks kissed sacred objects connected with some of their cults and the Arabs seem to have done the same from early times.

The forms of adoration developed in the cult of the emperors were chiefly of Persian origin. Not only bowing and genuflexion were customary, but kissing the robe, hand, foot, or knee of the emperor became common. And while these practices were more definitely established from the time of Diocletian, some of the previous emperors, for example Caligula and Elagabalus, had encouraged them.

Christian customs in prayer have undoubtedly been influenced by the pagan usages just mentioned. Here, however, as in so many other instances, we must guard against the assumption of an exclusively pagan source.

---

[3] *Verr.*, IV. 43. 94.

[4] I. 317. Merrill, however, in his note on the passage, expresses the opinion that the reference is not to kissing but to touching the hands of statues.

1. Posture in Prayer

THAT the early Christians stood while praying seems to be established from the pictures of persons praying (*orantes*) in the catacombs, and one cannot but feel that the Roman practice of standing during prayer has played some part in the determination of this attitude. On the other hand we must recognize the probability of Semitic influence, for the Hebrews stood when they prayed and Christ himself prayed standing. This posture still continues in the Lutheran Church and until recent times was usual among the Presbyterians.

The gesture of the raised hands found on Roman tombstones is reproduced in churches and tombs of the middle ages.[5]

The data available seem to indicate that the first Christians, like their pagan contemporaries, practiced kneeling only on occasions of unusual emotional stress. To be sure we are told in *Acts*[6] that both Peter and Paul knelt in prayer, and as the *Acts* were probably written about A.D. 80, this statement is of some significance for the custom at least in the latter

[5] Evans in *The Journal of Hellenic Studies*, VII, 47 (1886).

[6] 9.40, 20.36, 21.5. Cf. *Ephes.*, 3.14; *Phil.*, 2.10.

part of the first century. But there is no definite evidence at hand to prove satisfactorily
that this was the prevailing practice. The full
development of the custom of kneeling in prayer
came with the organization of the Protes-
tant churches after the Reformation. In the
Catholic Church it has always, to some extent
at least, involved the idea of penitence or urgent
supplication.

2. GRACE AT MEALS

THE custom of saying grace at meals was so
widely extended among the peoples who formed
the *milieu* in which Christianity developed (for
it was usual among the Greeks and Hebrews
as well as among the Romans) that its continuance by the early Christians was inevitable.
They had the institution indeed from the beginning. On the occasion of the feeding of the
five thousand Jesus kissed the loaves and fishes
and in the account of the miracle of the four
thousand we are told that He gave thanks.
There are numerous references to the custom
in the writings of the Church fathers.[7]

[7] *E. R. E.,* VI. 372.

3. KISSING SACRED OBJECTS

OF THE ancient custom of kissing sacred objects there are some survivals in our own time. The foot of the bronze statue of St. Peter in his basilica in Rome shows the attrition resulting from the kisses of countless worshippers. The rings of cardinals and the foot of the Pope are kissed by the devout. The kissing of the Bible in taking an oath is an obvious survival of this pagan practice. While these examples are in all probability immediately derived from Graeco-Roman culture, they may ultimately go back to some Oriental source. The tradition has indeed survived in the East as well as in Europe. The black stone of Mecca has been worn smooth by the kisses of countless generations of faithful Mohammedans, and this may reasonably be regarded as a survival of some earlier rite.

XXIV. SACRIFICE

THE ROMANS offered gifts of various kinds in honor of their gods, such as garlands, incense, lights, first-fruits, and cakes. They practiced animal-sacrifice extensively, and held sacramental meals through which they entered into communion with the gods. As examples of such meals may be mentioned the one celebrated on the Alban Mount on the occasion of the Latin Festival, when the delegates of the peoples belonging to the League participated in a meal in honor of Jupiter of the Latins (Iuppiter Latiaris) and by eating parts of the sacrificial victim entered into communion with him. Of a similar character were the sacramental banquets to Jove held during the Ludi Romani and the Ludi Plebeii on the Ides of September and November respectively. Mars and Silvanus were also honored in this way; and at the Feast of Ovens (Fornacalia), held in February, the gods were believed to participate in the meal that was given. A common meal formed part of the

ceremonies of the Arval Brothers. Meals were
also held in connection with the festivals of the
Parilia and Terminalia but the data are inadequate to enable us to determine whether they
were of a sacramental character or not. In
domestic worship the practice of offering to
the spirits of the household pieces of food from
the table indicates the belief that they were
present at the meal. Some scholars have
thought that these sacramental meals are the
oldest form of Roman sacrifice. However that
may be, they are undoubtedly of great antiquity.

Sacrifices were often made in expiation of
some offence. Any one who had violated the
sacred law (*ius divinum*) could re-establish
friendly relations with the gods only by making an expiatory sacrifice. Violations of this
law generally took the form of neglect or faulty
performance of some sacred rite. Acts of
penance for "sins" in our sense of the term
played no part in the old Roman religion.
They do, however, appear in connection with
some of the foreign cults that established themselves among the Romans. It is probable that
the idea was familiar to those under the influence of Orphic teaching, although we have no

detailed knowledge of the extent of Orphic influence. In the case of the cult of Isis, however, we know of the existence of the practice from Juvenal's [1] account of the women who were devotees of the goddess.

For expiatory sacrifices connected with the use of iron, see page 219.

Many offerings were made in fulfilment of vows (*ex voto*), which were common in both private and public life. The things vowed and, if the prayer were answered, subsequently dedicated to the god were of infinite variety, ranging from small objects of little intrinsic value to altars, shrines, and temples. It was customary for one depositing his offering in a temple to hang up there a tablet commemorating the circumstances of the vow. Horace [2] speaks of the person who having escaped shipwreck hung up the clothes he had worn, accompanied by a votive tablet to the god of the sea. A tablet of this kind on which was painted a picture of the event sometimes itself constituted the offering, and it is apparently to such paintings in temples of Isis that Tibullus and Juvenal allude.[3]

Cakes appear frequently in Roman ritual.

[1] VI. 522 ff.
[2] *Od.*, I. 5. 13–16. *Cf. Sat.*, II. 1. 33 and *A. P.*, 20.
[3] I. 3. 28; *Sat.*, XII. 28.

They are mentioned as offerings at the festival of the Liberalia [4] in March, at the Parilia [5] in April, at the Matralia [6] and the feast of Summanus in June, at the Feriae Sementivae (Paganalia) in January, and at the Fornacalia, Lupercalia, and Terminalia in February. In domestic worship also they had their place, and reference has already been made to the custom of making an offering to the household gods during dinner by throwing into the hearth-fire or placing on a movable altar a piece of the sacred salt-cake (*mola salsa*). Cakes in phallic shapes are also mentioned.[7]

Oil and honey were among the ingredients of the cakes used at the Liberalia, and Ovid gives us an interesting picture of the scene on the streets of Rome where old women who were called priestesses of Liber (*sacerdotes Liberi*) sold the cakes to passers-by. At every sale the vendor would break off a piece of the cake and offer it on a little altar that stood by her side. The sale seems to have been brisk, as well it might be when the purchaser got a cake and a hope of divine aid, all for a penny. The

[4] Ovid, *Fast.*, III. 725.
[5] *Ibid.*, IV. 743.
[6] *Ibid.*, VI. 482.
[7] Martial, XIV. 69.

[164]

cakes offered at the Parilia were of millet. Those used at the Matralia (*liba tosta*) were not baked but cooked in earthenware of a very primitive type. The cakes of wheat (*far*) offered at the Fornacalia were also made by some traditional process of great antiquity. Of especial interest are the cakes (*liba farinacea*) offered at the festival of Summanus, which were made in wheel-shaped moulds. And in this connection we should consider the moulds for sacred cakes described by Sir Arthur Evans in his article on " Recent Discoveries of Tarentine Terra-cottas." [8] That the objects he mentions are cake-moulds seems clear from the evidence he adduces, and we find on them, besides symbols of several gods, wheel and cross impressions. Moreover, some of the moulds are divided into segments and Evans plausibly suggests that the cakes were made in this way in order to facilitate distribution. In the British Museum also there are representations of round cakes, apparently used as offerings, which are divided into four parts, like the loaves found at Pompeii.

In the instances mentioned above the cakes themselves constituted the offerings. In other

[8] *The Journal of Hellenic Studies*, VII, 44 ff. (1886).

cases they were merely a concomitant of sacrifice. For example, pieces of sacred salt-cake (*mola salsa*) were regularly thrown on the head of the victim at a sacrifice. The head of the October Horse was decked with cakes before its immolation. A similar decoration appears on an occasion other than that of sacrifice in the case of the donkeys at the celebration of the festival of Vesta in June. The animals were probably so adorned because they turned the mills that ground the grain from which the bread was made.

A different use of cake in ritual is seen in the eating of the cake of *far* (*libum farreum*) by the bride and bride-groom at the ancient patrician marriage rite of *confarreatio*. The importance of this part of the ceremony is shown by the fact that it is from it that the name of the whole ceremony is derived. It seems to have been regarded as a sacrament through which the participating parties entered into a sort of communion with the god, called in this connection Iuppiter Farreus.

Only certain priests could officiate at the various acts of sacrifice, and membership in the priestly colleges generally involved the fulfilment of many conditions and sometimes the imposition of troublesome taboos. There were eleven colleges or organizations of priests, some of which included two or more groups. The higher magistrates also had sacerdotal powers; and in domestic religious services the head of the household (*paterfamilias*) officiated. It should be observed, however, that with some notable exceptions like the Vestals, a priestly office was not a full-time appointment. Membership in a priesthood did not exclude one from the ordinary activities of private or political life. On the other hand the priests of the Greek or Oriental cults adopted by the Romans frequently had no other occupation than that of the service of their divinity.

But it was not only the personnel of the priesthoods that was subject to strict regulations. Every detail in the ceremony of sacrifice must conform to sacerdotal prescription. Only those who were ceremonially clean could perform the act of sacrifice. Moreover, any divergence from the recognized ritual, any error on the part of the priest, any word or occurrence of ill-omen during the ceremony vitiated the sacrifice and involved the necessity of its repetition. It was probably to prevent the person officiating from hearing sounds of evil omen that his 'head was veiled.

Of these pagan ideas of sacrifice, some traces still exist:

1. CANDLES

CANDLES are burned in Catholic Churches in honor of saints or the Virgin Mary.

2. THE EUCHARIST

THE sacrifice of the Eucharist as celebrated in the Greek and Roman churches involves some of the beliefs inherent in the sacred meals mentioned in the preceding paragraphs, through which the pagan worshippers believed that they established communion with their gods. The Eucharist, however, cannot be said to be a direct descendant of any or all of the Roman sacramental meals. The evidence seems to indicate that the institution of the Last Supper was of Jewish origin, and was merely commemorative. On the other hand it seems probable that in the course of the centuries of conflict, under the influence not only of the conceptions implicit in the sacred meals of the Romans but also of those of Oriental cults like Mithraism, the sacramental idea of communion with God was more and more developed till it finally crystallized in the doctrine of transubstantiation. To attempt to specify a single source for this dogma is idle. The idea of entering into communion with gods through participating in meals at which they are believed to be present or through eating parts of victims which, having been sacrificed to them, are thought in a sense to be identified with them, may be found in the religions of many peoples. The records of anthropologists and students of comparative religion show how prevalent the idea of " eating the god " has been throughout the history of cults.[9]

3. EXPIATORY OFFERINGS

OF THE expiatory practices of early Roman religion there are no specific survivals in modern times, for the whole conception of what constitutes an offense to deity has changed. But on the other hand, while there is no specific survival, it can hardly be doubted that the rigid training which Romans received in the exact fulfilment of ritual requirements contributed substantially to the formation of a habit of mind that must needs continue to seek forgiveness for anything offensive in the sight

[9] Frazer, *G. B.*, VIII. 48 ff.

of God, even though the nature of the offense should be something wholly different. The maintenance of satisfactory relations with the divine powers — what the Romans called *pax deorum* — was an essential of pagan piety; it is also a large part of contemporary piety.

Of expiatory offerings or ceremonies in the foreign cults something more similar to survival may be found. For if we may assume that the Orphic propagandists of lower grade continued in Italy that traffic in remission of sins which Plato condemned, we have here a fore-shadowing of the abuse in indulgences which has so often been made the basis of attacks on the Catholic Church. Whatever the facts may be in regard to Orphic practice in Italy, there is no doubt about the matter so far as the priests of Isis are concerned. For Juvenal in the passage cited above represents an Egyptian priest as promising a woman that Osiris will grant her indulgence (*veniam*) for her son, if her bribe be adequate. The question of course arises whether this was a recognized part of the Isiac cult or whether it was merely a case of a delinquent priest. We have not sufficient data to decide definitely. That there were some excellent ethical elements in the

Egyptian cult we know from various passages
in Latin writers; [10] but it is equally true that
many of the priests were unscrupulous. In the
same way every one who has even a slight
knowledge of Roman Catholic doctrine knows
that the Church does not sell indulgences and
that her Councils have taken all kinds of precaution to prevent the abuse of them; but yet
it is equally certain that in the long history of
indulgences unscrupulous priests often have
sold them.

4. EX-VOTO OFFERINGS

OF THE pagan practice of affixing votive tablets to the walls of temples we have many survivals in the churches of Italy and other Catholic countries. At the fair held in connection
with the feast of SS. Cosma and Damiano at
Isernia in the Abruzzi many wax ex-votos were
sold to the devout and deposited by them in
the church.[11] And just as temples were often
erected by the Romans in fulfilment of vows,
so in modern times votive churches have been
built. One example is furnished by the Church
of St. Gennaro in Naples, which was vowed at
the time of a plague; [12] another is the Church

[10] For example, Tibullus, I. 3. 25; Juvenal, XIII. 92.
[11] See under Phallicism, page 76.
[12] Trede, *op. cit.*, I. 21.

of San Paolo in the same city, which was built by King Ferdinand early in the nineteenth century in accordance with a vow.[13]

5. SACRED CAKES

IT SEEMS probable that some of the Roman customs connected with sacred cakes have survived. For example, the hot cross buns that we eat on Good Friday have an obvious affiliation with the sacred cakes made in such moulds as those found at Tarentum. Again, the Simnel cakes eaten on Mid-lent Sunday are stamped with the figure of Christ or the Virgin Mary, replacing in all probability representations or symbols of pagan divinities. The marking of segments on some of the cakes used on festivals of the Christian year, as for example on Twelfth Day, certainly suggests the idea of distribution which has been mentioned as the probable reason for the dividing lines on the sacred cakes of the ancients. In the case of Twelfth cakes there seems to have been a part for every person in the house and for Christ, the Virgin, and the wise men from the East as well. And it is not too far a call to trace back to the sacred cake of the confarreate marriage

[13] *Ibid.*, I. 22.

in Rome the importance of the wedding-cake
in modern marriage.

Nor did the custom of offering cake or bread
as sacrifice pass away with paganism. We are
told [14] that in Franconia persons entering a forest make an offering of bread to the spirit of
the woods; and that in Bohemia bread is thrown
into a stream in which a man has been drowned.
In Devonshire offerings of pieces of cake, accompanied by libations of cider, used to be
made to the trees in the orchards.[15]

6. CEREMONIAL PARTICULARITY

OF THE Roman regulations covering the personnel of the priestly colleges, of their numerous prescriptions in regard to the ceremonial
cleanliness of those engaged in sacred offices,
and of the stress laid upon the performance
of sacrifices in exact conformity with ritual requirements there are doubtless traces in the emphasis laid on the importance of form and ritual
in some of our modern ecclesiastical systems.
They have survived even where the sacrifices
that once formed the most notable occasions for
their manifestation have passed away.

[14] Tylor, *Primitive Culture*, II. 195, 369.
[15] Chambers, *Book of Days*, I. 62–3; Brand, *op. cit.*,
I. 29 ff.; MacCulloch, *E. R. E.*, III. 60.

XXV. CEREMONIAL PROCESSIONS AND DANCES

1. PROCESSIONS IN ANCIENT AND IN MODERN TIMES

REFERENCE has already been made to the survival of Roman ceremonial processions in modern festivals of saints (see page 13), in marriage rites (page 33), in country-side " beating of the bounds " (pages 49 ff.), and in funerals (page 89). There was also the ceremony of the Amburbium, consisting of a procession around the bounds of the city with a view to its lustration and held annually on or about the second of February. One or two other examples may be mentioned. One of the spectacular ceremonies which the Romans adopted under Greek influence was the Supplication (*supplicatio*). It was resorted to in times of national danger or of public thanksgiving. The whole populace, both men and women, wearing garlands and carrying laurel-branches in their hands, took part under the direction of the priests in a procession that passed from temple to temple through the streets of Rome. If the occasion were one of national peril, the men made offerings of wine and incense at each temple where there was a pause, while the women, with hair down, knelt before the altars in supplication. If the occasion were a joyful one, prayers of thanksgiving and praise took the place of the petitions for divine aid.

We hear also of a processional rite first celebrated in 207 B.C. in expiation of an alarming prodigy. A choir of twenty-seven young women, accompanied by the members of the priestly College of Ten, marched from the temple of Apollo outside the Porta Carmentalis to the temple of Juno Regina on the Aventine. Pausing in the Forum they sang in honor of Juno a hymn which Livius Andronicus, one of the earliest of Latin poets, had composed. Other processions of girls are recorded, and it is to this type that the procession of twenty-seven boys and twenty-seven girls who sang Horace's *Carmen Saeculare* belongs.

There was, moreover, a ceremony of prayer for rain of which a procession was a notable feature. For in time of drought, at the bidding of the Pontiffs, the matrons with bare feet and flowing hair and the magistrates without the insignia of their office marched in procession through the city and prayed to Jupiter for rain.[1]

To these processions ordained on special occasions we see a striking resemblance in those *processiones extraordinariae* of the *Rituale Romanum*, either enjoined in time of war, plague, famine or *in quacumque tribulatione*, or ordered as a form of thanksgiving.[2]

2. THE SACRED DANCE OF THE ANCIENTS AND ITS SURVIVAL AMONG THE EARLY CHRISTIANS

CONNECTED with the procession in ancient times was the dance. In some ceremonies the two were combined as in the parade of the Salii, the priests of Mars. For when in the month of March the Salii, equipped as warriors, with shield in left hand and spear or staff in right, passed through the streets of Rome, they paused at various places and danced, striking their shield with the staff and singing their archaic song to Mars, the great spirit to

[1] Petronius, *Cen. Trimalch.*, 44.
[2] H. Thurston in *C. E.*, under " Processions," XII. 447.

whose power the quickening of vegetation in the spring was ascribed. Whether the leaping and dancing was supposed to accelerate the springing up of the crops as Frazer [3] has suggested or whether the clatter of the shields was intended to frighten away evil spirits who might injure the produce of the fields, it is hardly possible to say. There are, however, as every one will remember, plenty of parallels for the belief in the efficacy of noisy demonstrations in driving off mischief-making demons.

The dance appears in other forms of Roman ritual. The Arval Brothers danced as they chanted their song to Mars. The girl-choir referred to above accompanied their hymn to Juno with dance movements. Moreover, dances were characteristic of the cult of several of the foreign gods introduced into Rome, as for example, the Greek Bacchus, the Phrygian Cybele, the Cappadocian Ma-Bellona, and the Egyptian Isis.

The early Christians also recognized dancing as a form of worship. It is well-known that in the days of the primitive Church both bishops and people took part in dances before the tombs of martyrs and in churches. And there

[3] *G. B.*, II. 210.

[177]

is evidence that the ordinance of A.D. 692 forbidding the practice, was not successfully enforced. It is attested that even in the eighteenth century French priests in the provinces led sacred dances on saints' days.[4]

That any of the pagan Roman dances referred to contributed directly to the institution of the sacred dance among the Christians cannot be maintained. There is much more likelihood of direct influence from Jewish sources. The Jews, we know, practiced the sacred dance. David, to quote the most familiar example, "danced before the Ark," and we may be sure that his act was of religious significance, whether the idea was that of "moving" the god or something else. But while we cannot ascribe any direct influence to the Roman dances, it is equally obvious that they played their part in familiarizing the people with this form of sacred act and contributed indirectly to the establishment of the idea that dance-movements were an acceptable form of religious devotion.

[4] *Saturday Review,* 1896, 52.

XXVI. DIVINATION

1. The Liver and Other Parts of the Body

AMONG the Romans, seers known as *haruspices* divined the future by the examination and interpretation of the internal organs of sacrificial victims. These seers had originally been summoned from Etruria on special occasions but by the time of the Emperor Claudius a college of Roman *haruspices* had been organized.

They specialized in liver-lore, and to the importance they assigned this organ may be traced that belief in its magic powers that we find in the Middle Ages and in much later times. Mediaeval writers, for example, refer to the superstition that eating the liver of a goat enabled one to see in the dark. Vesalius speaks of the spirit that came from the liver. And the witches in *Macbeth* used the liver of a Jew in one of their magical concoctions. Superstitious Italians today believe that one may obtain magical power by eating a human liver.

Analogous to divination by the liver is the reading of bones of animals, especially the shoulder-blade of lambs and kids, so common in Macedonia and Albania today.[1] While this is not derived from the Etruscan or Roman liver-practice, it obviously had its origin in a similar attitude of mind. It survives in England in the reading of the speal-bone. Possibly here belongs also our use of the wishing-bone of a chicken, and the " merry thought " to which the person who gets the larger part is entitled.[2]

2. BIRDS

THE flight and notes of birds constituted an important part of the Roman augural system, and many modern superstitions connected with birds may be traced in part at least to Roman times. The geese that are kept in the precinct of the cathedral in Barcelona inevitably suggest the sacred geese of the temple of Juno Moneta on the Arx in ancient Rome. The hooting of owls, the croaking of ravens, the chattering of magpies have their significance for the superstitious in modern as in pagan

[1] Abbott, *Macedonian Folklore*, 96 ff.
[2] Wood-Martin, *Traces of the Elder Faiths of Ireland*, II. 141.

times. A sixth-century divining-rod, adorned with figures of birds, has been found near Ballymoney in County Antrim.[3] Our saying " A little bird has told me " finds its ultimate source in the ancient systems of bird-lore.

3. EARTHQUAKES

THE occurrence of an earthquake was almost universally regarded as a portent by the Romans as well as by many other peoples of ancient times. And there was sporadic expression of this old superstition among the illiterate on the occasion of the seismic disturbances in California in 1906.

4. ASTROLOGY

FURTHER, astrology appealed to many Romans. The attacks made on astrologers by Cato the Elder are a matter of record, and in 139 B.C. the feeling against them was so strong that they were banished from Italy by senatorial decree. But the law of exclusion was probably not enforced long. At any rate they were active in Rome in the beginning of the first century and their influence increased from that time. More and more persons believed

[3] Wood-Martin, *ibid.*, II. 143.

that the aspect of the heavens at the moment of their birth determined the events of their life. The general belief that Nigidius Figulus had successfully prophesied the career of Augustus by casting his horoscope undoubtedly had enormous influence in increasing the vogue of astrologers. Their art flourished all over the Empire.

These ideas were current in the early days of Christianity, flourished for a thousand years afterwards and have not entirely disappeared in modern times. When St. Matthew recorded the star in the east he was conforming to a widespread belief among both the Jews and the Gentiles of the period. In the Middle Ages the list of portents — eclipses of the sun and moon, spots on the sun, etc. — that warned the world of the impending death of Charlemagne inevitably reminds one of those lists of prodigies that appear so often in Livy's history of Rome. A French author, Pierre Bayle,[4] writing in the seventeenth century, protests against the superstitious ideas which many of his contemporaries had in regard to comets and eclipses. Of the part once played by astrology in popular belief we have relics in such English words as

[4] *Pensées diverses à l'occasion de la comète de 1680.*

jovial, martial, and saturnine. Moreover, newspapers still publish " daily horoscopes."

5. WATER

OF THE Roman practice of divining by water (*hydromantia*), of which St. Augustine [5] gives us an account, traces may still be found in the modern pretense of reading the future in tea leaves or coffee grounds. With us this is a mild form of afternoon-tea jesting, but the seriousness with which it was sometimes taken as late as the eighteenth century may be seen from the reference to the subject in the *Gentleman's Magazine* for March, 1731.

6. ORACLES AND RHAPSODOMANCY

ORACLES also were frequently consulted by the Romans in times of doubt or danger. Especially famous were the Sibylline verses, which were brought to Rome from Cumae in Campania toward the end of the regal period and deposited in the Capitoline temple of Jupiter. The Roman historians record many occasions on which the college of priests in charge of them was ordered by the Senate to search them for guidance. They played an important part

[5] *De civitate Dei*, VII. 35.

in the religious life of Rome and it was only in the fifth century after Christ that they were destroyed. There were other oracles in Italy also and we hear with special frequency of the lots (*sortes*) of the temple of Fortune in Praeneste. These consisted of small inscribed tablets or tokens of more of less general or ambiguous content in the interpretation of which the persons concerned had considerable range. The Romans consulted foreign oracles also, such as that of Apollo at Delphi and Zeus at Dodona.

Another way of reading the future was divination by books (rhapsodomancy). One would open a book at hazard and the first line the eye lighted on was regarded as an oracle. Homer was so used (*sortes Homericae*) and, according to Bouché-Leclercq, Hesiod also. Virgil's works were frequently employed in this way from the time of Hadrian (*sortes Virgilianae*).[6]

The early Christians seem to have believed in oracles as much as their pagan contemporaries. Their explanation of them, however, was different. They regarded them as the instruments of evil demons, as we see from the

---

[6] See Pease in note on Cicero, *De. div.*, I. 12.

statements of Ambrose, Jerome, and Augustine. At any rate these writers show no signs of believing that the oracles were manipulated by trickery. Some of the Christians thought that the Sibylline oracles had foreshadowed the coming of Christ, nor do they anywhere hint that such of these oracles as might bear this interpretation could have been inserted in the collection by some Christian whose honesty had yielded to the urge of his piety. Even a Christian emperor like Theodosius consulted pagan oracles and the extent to which the old practice was continued is shown by the number of prohibitory laws passed from the time of Theodosius to that of Justinian. In general, however, the policy of the Christians was to substitute oracles of their own for those of pagan origin. Intead of oracles connected with the shrine of some pagan god or demi-god we find oracles attached to the church or tomb of a saint. The Praenestine and the Virgilian lots yielded place to the lots of the Saints (*sortes Sanctorum*). A Bible would be placed on a saint's tomb and opened, and the first verse which one saw was accepted as a divine sign. Not that the use of Virgil's writings as oracles passed away entirely. Christians of the Middle

Ages sometimes sought guidance in them and Pease [7] cites an interesting example of survival in much later times. He tells us that King Charles I of England consulted Virgil in this way.

7. VISIONS

THE pagan belief in the validity of visions seen in dreams and trances recurs in a number of passages in the New Testament. St. Matthew [8] tells us of the dreams of Joseph and of Pilate's wife. In *Acts* [9] we hear of the trances of Peter and Paul.

8. CHRISTIAN ATTITUDE TOWARD DIVINATION

IN BRIEF, while the Christian attitude toward divination of all sorts may have been affected in some degree by considerations of policy — for any religious system that eliminated oracles and other supernatural manifestations would have suffered in that era of religious competition — the chief element in the situation seems to have been a genuine belief in the efficacy of supernatural signs. It is a belief of

[7] *Loc. cit.*
[8] I. 20; 2. 12, 13, 22; 27. 19.
[9] 10. 10; 22. 17. Cf. II *Cor.*, 12. 2.

unusual durability. Trede tells us of the prestige enjoyed in high places by the prophetess who truthfully foretold the return of Pope Pio Nono to Rome after his flight in 1849. Nor even in our own day are prophets and signs wholly without honor among some classes of society.

XXVII. SACRED EDIFICES: THEIR FORM, ORIENTATION AND CONSECRATION

1. ARCHITECTURAL FORM

ALTHOUGH temples of Roman or Graeco-Roman gods were frequently appropriated by the Christians and used as churches, their architectural plan had little or no influence on the form of the Christian church. The origin of the latter has been a subject of controversy for a long time, but now appears to be solved. This solution, however, is not to be found in the current theory that the Christian basilica is a development of the plan of the Roman house, either of the front part with its recess (*tablinum*) and central space (*atrium*), or of the inner part (*peristylum*) with its recess (*exedra*) and large open area with colonnades on either side.[1] The right explanation was first suggested by Ga-

[1] Lowrie, *Christian Art and Archaeology*, 94–101; Holborn in *E. R. E.*, I. 697.

briel Leroux,[2] who pointed out that the type
of the Christian basilica goes back to the sanctuaries used by the adherents of oriental cults.
As Bagnani[3] has shown, this theory seems
confirmed by the discovery in 1917 of the
subterranean basilica just outside the Porta
Maggiore in Rome. A glance at its plan with
atrium at the entrance, central hall and apse,
must bring home to every one the degree to
which it reveals the chief characteristics of the
early Christian churches. The presence of the
atrium is especially convincing. Bagnani aptly
compares this subterranean basilica with the
sanctuary of Mithras found under the garden
of the Baths of Caracalla, which with its ves-
tibule and columns supporting a vault offers
distinct points of resemblance. It is difficult
to date the sanctuary at the Porta Maggiore.
It may belong to the end of the first century.
Nor do we know what cult was practiced there,
although the stucco decorations make it clear
that the immortality of the soul was one of
its chief tenets. That it was one of the
oriental mystery religions seems probable.

[2] *Exploration archéologique de Delos,* II: "La salle
hypostyle."
[3] *The Journal of Roman Studies,* IX, 78–85 (1919).

Cumont,[4] however, thinks that it was the meeting place of a Neopythagorean sect.

2. ORIENTATION

VITRUVIUS [5] tells us that the Romans built their temples to face west so that the person standing before the altar would look east; and in such a system of orientation one might plausibly see the origin of the common plan of building churches with doors at the west end and altar at the east. But what we have learned from excavations in regard to the sites of Roman temples does not tend to confirm Vitruvius' statement. Assuredly if the Romans had such a rule as that indicated by him they regarded it as one more honored in the breach than in the observance. As a matter of fact it is extremely difficult to demonstrate any plan of orientation for Roman temples. Even Nissen's [6] elaborate theory that the orientation of

[4] *Rassegna d'arte antica e moderna,* XXI. 37–44.

[5] IV. 5: aedis signumque . . . spectet ad vespertinam caeli regionem, uti qui adierint ad aram . . . spectent ad partem caeli orientis et simulacrum. Hyginus, *De lim. const.* (I. p. 169 in edition of Agrimensores by Blume, Lachmann and Rudorff), says something of the same kind but confines the practice to the earlier period.

[6] *Templum,* 162; also in *Rhein. Mus.,* XXVIII. 513–57; XXIX. 369–433; XL. 38–65, 329–70; XLII. 28–61; and in *Orientation,* 298 ff. See Wissowa's note, *R. u. K.,* 472 A[1].

a temple was determined by the position of the rising sun on the day of the foundation is confronted by many difficulties.

We seem to be on surer ground when we turn to the Greek and Roman temples in Asia, for although there were notable exceptions, most of these had their door at the east end and the image of the god at the west. It has been claimed by some that the early Christians adopted this system and that the orientation of St. Peter's basilica in Rome goes back to this tradition. But whether the church with east door and west altar was the original one or not, it is quite certain that later the regular system of orientation was that with west door and east altar. This system established itself in the eastern Church earlier than in the western. Indeed there is some probabilty that the western Church objected to it as too suggestive of the practice of the numerous sun-cults whose adherents turned to the rising sun in prayer and adoration. Finally, however, the western Church followed the example of the eastern and the orientation with west door and east altar became fairly general.

What was the ultimate significance of this orientation? Was it due to the influence of

sun-worship? Cults of the sun, as we know
from many sources, had attained great vogue
during the second, third, and fourth centuries.
Sun-worshippers indeed formed one of the big
groups in that religious world in which Christianity was fighting for a place. Many of them
became converts to Christianity and in all
probability carried into their new religion some
remnants of their old beliefs. The complaint
of Pope Leo in the fifth century that worshippers in St. Peter's turned away from the altar
and faced the door so that they could adore
the rising sun is not without its significance in
regard to the number of Christians who at one
time had been adherents of some form of
sun-worship. It is of course impossible to say
precisely in what way their influence manifested itself. We do know, however, of ana-
logues between Christ and the sun; he was
designated the Sun of Righteousness; and our
Christmas falls on the date of the festival of
a popular sun-god in Rome.[7] On the whole
sun-worship seems to have been the chief influence in determining the prevailing form of
church-orientation. It was not however the
sole influence. The sun-worshippers were not

[7] See pp. 150–53.

[192]

the only ones who turned to the east in prayer.
The Romans had done this even in the early
days of their history, long before Oriental sun-
cults had been introduced among them. This
position is directly attested for the Master of
the Arval Brothers, and many other examples
might be cited.[8] It is reasonable to suppose
that some of those Christians who were com-
pared by Tertullian[9] to sun-worshippers because they turned toward the east in prayer
had never had any affiliations with sun-worship, but in looking east were merely adhering
to the old Roman ritual in which they had
been brought up.

3. CONSECRATION

THE Romans used to consecrate their temples
and it was customary to hold a festival on the
day of consecration. In a great many cases
the festival had been celebrated prior to the
building of the temple, but when under the influence of Greek religion temples were erected,
the dedication day of the temple was made to
coincide with the date of the ancient festival of

[8] See *Aen.*, VIII. 68, XII. 172; Ov., *Fast.*, IV. 777; Val.
Flacc., *Argon.*, III. 437.
[9] *Apol.*, 16.

the god. By the act of consecration the temple became the possession of the divinity and any one who violated its sanctity was subject not to civil but to sacred law. Not only temples, but altars and statues were consecrated.

While the custom of dedicating a temple and of holding a festival on the anniversary of the dedication is not confined to the Romans — for the Jews consecrated the Temple in Jerusalem and regularly celebrated the anniversary of the ceremony — it seems probable that the Christian custom of consecrating churches is derived from the Romans. About the precise source of the Catholic form of consecration, however, there has been a good deal of discussion. The ceremony consists in the consecrating priest's making a St. Andrew's cross on the pavement of the church by sprinkling ashes. This, according to some, goes back to the cross drawn by a Roman augur in marking out a temple. Others see in it a reminiscence of the methods of Roman surveyors but explain the cross as a representative of the initial letter of Christ's name in Greek (X).[10] The plausibility of this explanation of the cross does not

[10] de Rossi, *Bull. arch. christ.*, 1881, 140; Duchesne, *Christian Worship*, 417.

preclude the high probability of the act of consecration as a whole being of Roman origin.

Of the relation of Christian dedication-day celebrations to pagan festivities we have some records for England.[11]   For when the Anglo-Saxons were converted to Christianity, Pope Gregory the Great instructed the abbott Mellitus who had participated in the mission to the island, not to prohibit the pagan festivals but to tell the people to erect their booths around the temples which had now been turned into Christian churches and to celebrate the anniversary of the dedication of the church or the birth of the martyr for whom it had been named.[12]   The celebrations — wakes, as they were called — continued for centuries in England.   When early in the seventeenth century an attempt was made to suppress them, King Charles I interfered and ordered their continuance.   In the northern counties of England these feasts have not yet been abolished.   The " Patron's Day " celebration in Ireland belongs to the same class of festival.

[11] Brand, *op. cit.*, II. 2 ff.
[12] Brand, *ibid.:* ut die dedicationis vel nataliciis sanctorum martyrum, tabernacula sibi circa easdem ecclesias, quae ex fanis commutatae sunt, de ramis arborum faciant. (Bed., I. 30).

Finally it may be noted that the modern practice of dedicating buildings other than churches (for example college, lodge or club buildings) is derived from the same ancient observance.

XXVIII. RELIGIOUS USAGES
COMMON TO PAGANS
AND CHRISTIANS

1. HOLY WATER

THE LUSTRAL use of water was familiar to the Romans at an early date. Livy[1] records an incident of the time of King Servius which presupposes a belief in the necessity of ablution before sacrifice. In many cases a laurel-branch, dipped in water, was used to sprinkle a place or object that needed lustration.[2] Tacitus[3] speaks of the lustration by means of water of the site of the Capitoline temple of Jove on the occasion of its rebuilding in the time of the Emperor Vespasian. And Tertullian[4] mentions the purification of residences, temples, and whole cities

---

[1] I. 45. 6: "Quidnam tu, hospes, paras" inquit "inceste sacrificium Dianae facere? Quin tu ante vivo perfunderis flumine?"

[2] Ov., *Fast.*, IV. 728; V. 677.

[3] *Hist.*, IV. 53.

[4] *De Baptismo*, 5.

by the same method. There is, however, no evidence that water was used on the *dies lustricus* — the ninth day after birth in the case of a boy and the eighth in that of a girl — when a child was given its name. It is difficult to see on what grounds the statement is made that on this occasion " the child was passed through water." [5] Macrobius [6] refers to some kind of lustration but he does not specify water.

In some of the Oriental cults established in Rome and elsewhere in Italy holy water had a still more important part. It was for example a feature of the cult of Isis, as is shown by the fresco of Herculaneum referred to on page 134. Moreover, one of the buildings in the precinct of the Isiac temple at Pompeii contains a tank apparently intended for the storage of the holy water from the Nile. Further, we know from Apuleius [7] that baptism by the priest was a prerequisite for initiation into the mysteries of Isis, its purpose being purification and remission of sins. The worshippers of Sabazios also, a Thraco-Phrygian deity known in Rome at least by the end of the second century, were

[5] *E. R. E.,* under " Baptism."

[6] *Sat.,* I. 16. 36: est autem lustricus dies, quo infantes lustrantur et nomen accipiunt.

[7] *Met.,* XI. 23: sacerdos . . . me . . . abluit.

baptized before initiation. And the followers of the Mithras cult also practiced baptism.

The examples I have cited both from early Roman practice and from the Oriental religions show how common the ritual use of water among the pagans was. And while it cannot be maintained that the Christians derived their rite of baptism from this source — for it is much more probable that the dominating influence was the Jewish practice — yet it may reasonably be said that the stress laid upon the rite by so many pagan cults and the strength of its appeal to the masses, who doubtless found a special satisfaction in the simplicity of its symbolism, contributed materially to the institution of the Christian doctrine.

The ancient Roman custom of touching a baby's forehead and lips with spittle on the day on which it received its name is mentioned by Persius [8] with caustic comment. The purpose of the act apparently was to avert the machinations of witch or demon.[9] A similar use of spittle survives in the baptism service of the Roman Church today, in which the

[8] *Sat.*, 2. 31.

[9] The subject is discussed by Nicolson in his article "The Saliva Superstition" in *Harvard Studies in Classical Philology*, VIII. 23–40 (1897).

priest touches the ears and nostrils of the candidate for baptism with spittle, using among other phrases the words: *tu autem effugare, diabole*. Doubtless the immediate source of the Catholic usage is St. Mark's [10] account of Christ's cure of the deaf-and-dumb man. But the Roman belief in the efficacy of spittle against malign influences was also an element in the establishment of the practice.

2. MUSIC

SONG was a very old tradition in Roman cult, and chants of religious content in the primitive Italian measure constituted some of the earliest attempts of the Romans in the field of lyric poetry. Examples are the songs of the Arval Brothers and of the Salii. We have evidence also of a lyrical element in supplications addressed to other gods.[11] Moreover, flutists regularly played during sacrifices and took part in many other religious ceremonies. It has been maintained by some that the original purpose of this music was to drive away evil spirits.[12] Others have thought that it was used

[10] 7. 33, 34.
[11] R. Peter, " De Romanorum precationum carminibus " in *Commentationes in honorem A. Reifferscheidii*, 67–83.
[12] Granger, *The Worship of the Romans*, 283.

in order to prevent the person performing the sacrifice from hearing any words of ill-omen. Whatever its origin, there developed in the course of time adequate realization of its effectiveness in inducing a feeling of piety and in intensifying religious emotion. This was manifestly the idea that motivated the greatly increased emphasis on music that marked all ceremonies that were conducted in accordance with the forms of Greek ritual, and the popularity of Greek rites grew steadily from the early days of the Republic. To Greek influence for instance must be attributed the use of the lyre in sacred ceremonies, although this instrument established itself so slowly that Horace [13] speaks of its use in religious service as something relatively new in his time.

But other causes besides the growing popularity of Greek ritual were operating to give greater prominence to the musical element in worship. Music was one of the most striking features of the Oriental cults that from the end of the third century before Christ till the third or fourth century of our era played so im-

[13] *Od.*, III. 11. 3: Tuque, testudo . . . , Nec loquax olim neque grata, nunc et Divitum mensis et amica templis.

portant a part in Roman religious history. The street processions of the priests of the Great Mother were accompanied by the beating of tambourines, the blaring of horns, and the clashing of cymbals. Inscriptions referring to the cult indicate an elaborate musical personnel: drummers, players of cymbals, flutists, and hymnists. In the worship of Isis music was one of the most important elements. A notable feature of the November festival was the choral ode sung by a choir of twenty-seven members. In the processions both vocal and instrumental music were employed. Now it was the rattle of the *sistrum,* now the flute, now the voices of choirs of young people, clad in white robes, who sang the praises of Isis or Serapis.[14] But wildest of all cult-music was that of the priests of Ma-Bellona, the Cappadocian goddess, as they paraded to the accompaniment of trumpet and tambourine.

Such was the tradition of religious music into which Christianity in Rome was born. At first many of the Christians, associating music with all that was pagan, were bitterly opposed to it and we find writers of the fourth and fifth centuries condemning the use of song

[14] Apul., *Met.,* XI. 9.

and instruments in cult. So rigid an attitude, however, could hardly have been universal even in the early days, especially in the matter of vocal music. The earliest Christians used song in worship as we know from the New Testament, and there was besides the inevitable influence of the Jewish use of instrumental music in cult. St. Ambrose, toward the end of the fourth century, is said to have introduced the chanting of psalms by responsive choirs and St. Gregory the Great, who lived two centuries later, is credited with the institution of a musical ritual for the churches of Rome. But the whole question of the steps in the transition from classical to Christian music is involved in obscurity. The extensive use of music in many of the cults practiced in Rome must have had some influence on the Christians in the organization of their service; it is probable also that even such early Christian music as the Ambrosian chants may have perpetuated the tradition of some Greek or Graeco-Roman melody. But too little is known about the nature of the original Ambrosian or Gregorian music to justify a positive statement. Even the relation of what is now called Ambrosian or Gregorian music to the original systems of the two bishops is a matter of great uncertainty.

3. BELLS, GONGS, RATTLES

THE use of bells in religious services was common in India and China long before it was adopted in Europe. We have, however, some fairly early examples in Greece and Etruria. For we are told that at the sanctuary of Zeus at Dodona bells were rung or gongs sounded; and the tomb of the Etruscan prince Porsenna, near Clusium, was equipped with a number of little bells that vibrated in the wind. On Roman soil we hear of a gong at the second temple of Jupiter Capitolinus, dedicated by Catulus in 69 B.C. Its purpose, like that of the bells at Dodona and on Porsenna's tomb, was probably to frighten away malicious spirits.

Bells were used in some of the foreign cults introduced into Italy. For example in the Bacchanalia both Bacchants and Bacchantes sometimes carried a bell in their hand or had one tied to their wrist or fastened on the thyrsus. The priests of the Great Mother and Attis also made use of bells, as is shown by the bas-reliefs connected with this cult in which a number of small bells are seen suspended from the branches of a tree. In the cult of Isis the rattle (*sistrum*) was in constant use both in processions and in services at the temple. In these cases also the most probable explanation of the practice is the belief that the sound warded off evil demons.

Of this prophylactic use of bells there are still other examples. The inscription on a small gold bell that was dug up on the Esquiline Hill in Rome makes definite reference to the evil eye. Probably the bells sometimes attached to the car of a general celebrating a triumph were intended to furnish protection against malign influences. And the same may be said of the bells so often hung on the head or neck of horses and other animals in Roman times. One of the mules in Phaedrus' fable [15] and the ass in Apuleius' *Metamorphoses* [16] wore a bell.

From more than one Latin author we know that the ringing of bells and the sounding of gongs were among the noises used to drive away the evil spirit that caused an eclipse.[17]

It is doubtful whether executioners or the criminals whom they executed wore bells, as

[15] II. 7 (Muli duo et latrones).

[16] X. 18: tintinnabulis perargutis exornatum.

[17] Juvenal, VI. 441 ff. Cf. Liv., XXVI. 5; Tac., *Ann.*, I. 28. 3.

has sometimes been claimed. Certainly the passages cited from Plautus [18] in support of the contention do not furnish adequate evidence.

Of special interest for our study is a bell found at Tarragona in Spain. It belonged to one Felix, a slave in a temple of the city, who used it in the rites of the cult of the Emperor (*sacris Augustis*). He may have rung it to indicate the moment of sacrifice or some other important point in the ritual.

Of these Roman examples of the use of bells there are some survivals. Certainly the bells that one sees today on the harness of horses in Italy go back to the ancient practice of which some instances have been given above. In Italy, especially among the lower classes, there is still belief in and fear of the evil eye, witchcraft, and other hostile influences of superhuman character.

And it is likely that in the use of the bell found at Tarragona to which reference has just been made we have the origin of the custom of ringing a small bell (the *sanctus*) at the celebration of the mass. Apparently an analogous use was made of the *sistrum* by the priests of Isis. In the fresco from Herculaneum de-

[18] *Pseud.*, 332; *Truc.*, 782.

picting the adoration of the holy water the priest and priestess on either side of the officiant are represented as shaking a *sistrum*. It is to this use of the *sistrum* that some scholars attribute exclusively the ringing of the bell in the ceremony of the mass, but the analogy is not sufficiently close to justify this conclusion.

There were probably other uses of bells in the earlier days of the Church. We have for example an illustration in which St. Patrick is represented in the act of giving a bell to a bishop on his consecration as if it were an essential of his office. We may assume also that the pagan practice of ringing bells to ward off evil spirits did not pass away with the establishment of Christianity. It may have contributed to the ringing of bells at funerals so often attested in mediaeval times. Tyack [19] in his comments on the representation of the funeral of Edward the Confessor draws attention to the two boys attending the corpse, each of whom is ringing a pair of handbells. He says that this practice was derived from paganism. To a certain extent this may be true. Probably the ringing of the bells by the boys was intended to protect the dead king from evil spirits. We

[19] *A Book About Bells.*

know that the Romans sometimes blew horns
and beat tambourines when a soul was passing,[20] and the idea may have been similar.
That evil spirits prowled around the dying and
might injure the dead seems to have been a
widely accepted belief. The original significance of the "passing-bell" in England is certainly the same as that of the horn and tambourine just mentioned.

The ringing of bells to summon people to
worship was a development of the Christian
era. There is no evidence of such a custom
among the Romans in pagan times, nor is it
likely that the Christian practice was instituted
till after the persecutions had ceased. It is
probable that it is not earlier than the fourth
century.

4. LIGHTS

LIGHTED lamps and torches appear in various
cults and ceremonies of ancient Rome. The
women who marched in procession from Rome
to the sanctuary of Diana on Lake Nemi carried torches. Lights too were used in rites connected with the dead. One of the reliefs on the
monument of the Haterii now in the Lateran

---

[20] See fig. 3358, Daremberg et Saglio, *Dictionnaire,*
under *Funus.*

Museum shows lighted lamps at the head and foot of the corpse; and lamps, placed in or near tombs, were lighted on certain occasions. Moreover, there can be little doubt that lights had an important part in the ritual of several of the Greek and Oriental divinities in Rome. The torch was one of the symbols of Ceres (Demeter), and the lamps found in one of the rooms in the precinct of Isis in Pompeii were doubtless used with symbolical significance in the cult of the Egyptian goddess. Further, the polemical writings of Tertullian (about A.D. 200) and Lactantius (about A.D. 300) make it plain that the placing of lights before the images of gods and on votive objects was a common pagan practice.

At first the Christians scrupulously refrained from a ritual use of lights. In their eyes apparently the practice had the taint of paganism. But from the end of the third century their attitude seems to have changed and after the recognition of Christianity by Constantine the symbolical use of lights established itself firmly in many kinds of ceremonies. Candles were burned before images of the Madonna or Christ or the Saints, and were a conspicuous part of numerous ceremonial processions and sacred ceremonies such as baptisms, marriages, and funerals. While some of the Christian writers continued to protest against this pagan element in the Church, others defended it.[21] Lights became and still are an inevitable concomitant of many forms of religious service. Their reintroduction into cult after the primitive simplicity of the first few centuries of Christianity had passed away, was only one phase of that externalism that came to be a notable characteristic of Christianity after and partly as a result of the imperial favor which it attained.

5. INCENSE

LIVY [22] speaks of a ceremony in Rome in 296 B.C. at which incense (*tus*) was used; Plautus [23] mentions an offering of incense and wine to the Lar of the family; and Cato [24] specifies a similar offering to Janus, Jove, and Juno. In view of this it is probable that Arnobius [25] and Ovid [26] overstressed the lateness of the date of its introduction among the Romans. In any

[21] Cf. Hieronymus, II. 2: Illud fiebat idolis et idcirco detestandum est; hoc fit martyribus et idcirco recipiendum est.

[22] X. 23. 2.

[23] *Aul.*, 24.

[24] *De agric.*, 141.

[25] VII. 26.

[26] *Fast.*, I. 341.

case it is clear that even if they did not have
incense proper in their early days they had
some other fragrant material that served the
same purpose. Its use doubtless increased with
the growth of Greek influence in Roman ritual,
and among other occasions it was offered lavishly at *supplicationes*. In the days of religious conflict the practice of burning incense
distinguished pagans from Christians. Pru-
dentius calls the pagan idolaters " the incense-
bearing crowd " (*turifera grex*), and one of the
tests imposed on persons suspected of being
Christians was the offering of a few grains of
incense on the altar of some Roman god. St.
Cyprian [27] applies the term " incense-offerers "
(*turificati*) to Christians who recanted.

Perhaps it was the bitter associations of the
Christians with incense that inhibited its use
by them during the first four centuries of the
Church. At any rate there is no evidence of its
being employed ritually till nearly the end of
the fourth century. At that time there is a
reference to its use in a church in Jerusalem.
In the sixth century it is attested for Antioch,
and by the eighth century we hear of censers
being swung in western churches during the

[27] *Ep.*, 55. 1.

[211]

procession from the sacristy to the altar. Only gradually was its use extended in the west to the celebration of the mass and other solemn services of the Catholic church. This had, however, become the practice by the fourteenth century and now obtains. In the Anglican church the use of incense, which was abolished at the Reformation, was resumed about the middle of the nineteenth century and at present is increasing.[28]

6. VEILING

REFERENCE has already been made to the veiling of the bride (page 30) and to the custom of the celebrant's covering his head during sacrifice (page 168). Another notable example of veiling is attested for the Romans. For when the priests of Jupiter, Mars, and Quirinus sacrificed to Good Faith (Fides) on the Capitol on the first of October, their right hands were wrapped in white cloth. The uniqueness of this ritual — for it does not occur in the cult of any other Roman divinity — shows that the idea was not so much that of approaching the goddess with clean hands as that of safe-guard-

[28] Athcley, *History of the Use of Incense in Divine Worship.*

ing and preserving the purity and sanctity of the right hand which was regarded by the Romans as the abiding-place of Good Faith. For they too clasped their right hands when they made pledges. That this is the dominant conception of the act seems clearly indicated by Livy.[29] There is no evidence that the right hand of the statue of Fides was also covered, as Fowler has suggested on the basis of a passage in Horace.[30] The poet has probably transferred to the goddess the attribute of the priests.

But while the ultimate explanation of the covering of the hand is such as has been described, the act also came to connote respect and homage, and of this aspect of it we have survivals. In Christian art the hands of Peter receiving the keys are sometimes represented as covered. There are pictures also of martyrs holding their crowns with veiled hands. And in our own time cardinals have their hands covered when they receive the hat from the Pope and when they approach him to do homage.

[29] I. 21. 4: significantes fidem tutandam, sedemque eius etiam in dextris sacratam esse.
[30] *Od.*, I. 35. 21–22: albo . . . Fides . . . velata panno.

7. GARLANDS

GARLANDS were extensively used in Roman religious rites.[31] They were put on statues of the gods, were worn by worshippers, formed part of the equipment of bride and groom at wedding ceremonies, and were even placed on the heads of the dead. Whether the original idea was that the garland was a magic circle which protected from evil influences that which it encircled, cannot be stated positively. This explanation suits some of its uses, but in others the notion involved seems to be that of devoted adherence to divinity or cult or religious system.

In the early days of the Church the garland was a symbol of paganism, as is clear from Tertullian's [32] story of the soldier whose adherence to Christianity was detected through his refusal to wear one. The more rigid Christians carefully avoided chaplets and wreaths of all kinds in religious rites and ceremonies. Tertullian, Clement of Alexandria, and Cyprian are outspoken in their condemnation and denounce them as emblems of heathenism and all

[31] Köchling, *De coronarum apud antiquos vi atque usu*, 33 ff.
[32] *De corona*, 1.

that was bad in pagan practice. But little by
little the attitude of the Christians changed.
It was pointed out that more than one passage
in the Scriptures referred to " the crown of
life." [33] Moreover, chaplets were used by the
Gnostics in their mystic rites, and in the baptismal ceremony of the Coptic and Aethiopian
Christians a garland of myrtle and palm leaves
was placed on the head of the baptized. To
these Christian sects the wreath, like the girdle
which they also put on the person baptized,
probably symbolized consecration and complete devotion to God.

Of the ancient use of garlands in connection
with the dead we have traces of survival not
only in the almost universal funeral wreath
but also in the frequent sculptured representations of garlands on sepulchral monuments.

Nor is the Roman custom of decking statues
of gods with chaplets entirely gone. For the
same spirit that in Horace's ode [34] " crowned
the little images of the gods with rosemary and
myrtle " still finds expression in the images
of the Madonna decked with garlands that

[33] *Revelation,* 2. 10; *James,* 1. 12; I. *Peter,* 5. 4.
[34] III. 23. 15–16.

may be seen along the roads in southern Italy.[35]

8. Tonsure

THE shaven head was one of the characteristics of the priests of Isis. Moreover, the shaving of the head was a necessary preliminary to initiation into the mysteries of the Egyptian goddess. The Isiac custom probably had a certain degree of influence on the attitude of the early Christians toward the practice and had something to do with the later adoption of the tonsure by priests and monks. But the influence was neither immediate nor direct nor exclusive. Tonsure was known to other Oriental religions besides Isiaism and Christianity. It was practiced by the Hebrews, and its existence in Brahmanic and Buddhist rites may indicate a long anterior history in the Far East.

There is no evidence that it was extensively practiced in the early days of the Church. To be sure both Peter and Paul are said to have had tonsured heads, and of its occasional use there seem to be clear indications in the New Testament. Perhaps the references in the lat-

[35] Trede, *op. cit.*, IV. 208; MacCulloch, in *E. R. E.*, IV. 340.

ter point only to special penitential occasions. But even so they are significant of a tendency and the oft-quoted saying of St. Jerome [36] that Christian priests should not appear with shorn head lest they be confounded with priests of Isis and Serapis or other heathen deities suggests the possibility that Christian clerics had sometimes done so. One gets the same impression from the action of the Council of Carthage (398), which prohibited the cutting of the beard and hair. It is a mistake to say that the tonsure was not practiced in the fourth century. All that can be safely said is that it was not authorized.

In heathen and Christian rites the significance of the tonsure was the same. It indicated the separation of the devotee from the world and his ascription to divine service. The practice probably first grew up among the Christians as a form of penitential devotion, to the development of which such customs as those of the Nazarites as described in the Old Testament [37] and those referred to in *Acts* [38] and in the *First Epistle to the Corinthians* [39] as well as the example of the priests and initiates of Isis

[36] In *Ezech.*, 44.   [38] 21. 24–26.
[37] *Numbers*, 6. 18.   [39] 11. 14, 15.

made their respective contributions. It was firmly established among orders of monks as early as the fifth century.

9. KNOTS

A ROMAN bride always wore at her wedding a girdle tied with a "Herculean knot" (*nodus Herculaneus*). After the ceremony was over and she had been escorted to her new home, this knot was loosed in the bridal chamber by her husband. So closely associated with the marriage rite was this tying and untying of the girdle that both processes were believed to be under the direct supervision of Juno, goddess of marriage and childbirth, sometimes called on account of her connection with this custom "Juno of the Girdle" (*Iuno Cinxia*). The symbolism shifts from the permanence of the marriage bond indicated by the tying of the knot to the removal of restrictions signified by its untying.

Of this Roman "knot of Hercules" there may be, as has been suggested,[40] a survival in the modern love-knot, which is regarded as an emblem of true and abiding affection. Possi-

[40] Thomas Browne, *Works* (London edition of 1904), II. 366.

bly, however, the latter is a parallel rather than a survival.

Ovid tells us that a pregnant woman must undo her hair before praying to the spirits of childbirth and that she must not have any knots in her clothing. Dilling [41] cites a parallel to this in Bilaspur, where women's hair must never be knotted during childbirth; and the same writer draws attention to the fact that in some Jewish communities, when there is a difficult labor in the house, the unmarried girls let down their hair.

10. TABOO ON IRON

THERE was a taboo on iron among the Romans as well as among other ancient peoples. If the Arval Brothers ever used an iron tool within the precincts of their sacred grove, they were obliged to make a piacular sacrifice. The high-priest of Jupiter (*flamen Dialis*) could not be shaved or shorn with an iron razor or shears, and some Sabine priests seem to have been subject to a similar restriction. No iron was used in the building or repairing of the Pons Sublicius, which was the oldest bridge across the Tiber and always had sacred associations for

[41] *E. R. E.,* VII. 748.

the Romans. An iron plough could not be used in marking the sacred boundary (*pomerium*) of a newly-founded city. The same attitude toward this metal is seen in the fact that it was only by special provision that the temple of Iuppiter Liber at Furfo could be repaired with iron tools. We are told also that cutting with an iron knife impaired the medicinal efficacy of mistletoe.[42]

There are traces of this taboo among the Greeks and Hebrews also. The council-chamber at Cyzicus on the Propontis was constructed entirely of wood without any nails, nor was any iron used in the temple at Jerusalem. But the fear of this metal was still more widespread than this. It probably existed among the Hindoos and numerous tribes of Europe, Africa, and North America. The taboo is probably to be traced back to the time when iron was a new discovery and therefore subject to suspicion.

There are survivals of this superstition and though they cannot be said to be descended directly from the Roman tradition they are traceable to a psychological complex to which Roman religious belief made its contribution. Some of the most notable of these survivals are

[42] Pliny, *N. H.*, XXIV. 4. 6. 12.

found among the Highlanders of Scotland.[43] For example, when making a need-fire these Scots take special precautions to have nothing made of iron on their persons. Similarly no iron is ever used by them in making a Yule-tide fire-wheel. Nor will they put iron in the ground, either to dig a grave or plough a field, on Good Friday. Taboos of the same kind are observed in the Hebrides. In Russia wizards who use the plant called loose-strife in the practice of their art never cut it with an iron knife. The introduction of iron ploughs into Poland aroused the superstitious fears of the peasants and furnished them with an explanation for bad crops. Other examples of taboo on iron are cited by Frazer [44] from Africa, Madagascar, Corea, and North America.

[43] Frazer, *G. B.*, III. 229.
[44] *Ibid.*, 225 ff.

XXIX. THE IDEA OF
REGENERATION

WHILE the idea of regeneration is not
stressed in the old Roman religion,
it is a mistake to suppose that it
appears only with the cults imported from
Greece and the Orient. It is true that the
dominant place occupied by it in some of the
foreign cults resulted in a reconstruction of religious thought, which, especially in regard to
the spiritual experience of individuals, marks
an epoch in the history of religion. But even
in the early religious observances of Rome there
were practices the whole purpose of which was
the attainment of that communion with deity
which is a basal element in all doctrines of regeneration. Examples may be found in the
sacred meals connected with the worship of
some Roman gods (page 161). But while the
idea of communion emerged here, it failed to
develop into a medium of personal regeneration.
It did not develop at all. Roman religion
passed more and more under the sway of sacer-

dotalism, and people came to think of the flaw-
less performance of rites as the chief means
of religious efficacy.

Doubtless this failure of Roman religion
to satisfy the religious longings of individuals had much to do with the success of
the emotional cults from the East that beginning at the end of the third century before Christ continued to invade Rome for five
hundred years. Several of these cults stressed
the idea of regeneration and the ultimate attainment of perfect spiritual purity and eternal
felicity in a world beyond the grave. Some of
the more important phases of this attitude as it
manifested itself in the different cults have already been touched upon in a previous chapter.
It has been pointed out, for example, that in the
worship of the Great Mother a person who had
participated in the *taurobolium* was believed
to be reborn (page 125). And this idea was
emphasized to such a degree that devotees after
taking part in the rite were not infrequently
treated like infants and their diet restricted for
some time to milk. Moreover, the whole story
of Attis, the associate of the Great Mother,
bears immediately on the doctrine of regeneration. Originally symbolizing the vegetation

that dies in the autumn and revives in the spring, he came to be a symbol of that spiritual rebirth that all true followers of the cult might aspire to. Such information as we have about the rite of the pine-tree — felled, carried into the temple, and regarded as Attis himself — shows clearly that all those who attended were believed to participate in the regenerative process so dramatically represented.[1] And the regeneration held for the next world as well as for this. In a word, Attis was a redeemer god.

Initiation into the mysteries of Isis, as we know from Apuleius, involved a baptism that washed away the impurities of man's imperfect nature and made him fit to commune with God. It is of especial interest that the same word "reborn" (*renatus*) is used by Apuleius of the initiate of Isis as by the followers of the Great Mother when they wrote the text of the inscriptions recording the *taurobolia*. The new life manifested itself in chastity and devotion to the service of the goddess. Faithful adherence to the doctrines of the cult assured the initiate not only happiness in this life but also everlasting felicity in the next; he was reborn to righteousness during his mortal span and to

[1] Willoughby, *Pagan Regeneration*, 122.

immortality under the benign favor of the goddess. A dramatic representation of the resurrection of Osiris, the husband of Isis, was part of the mysteries of the cult and in this the devotees were taught to see the assurance of their own resurrection to eternal life.[2] For Osiris also was a redeemer god.

In Mithraism (page 146) the idea of regeneration is still more prominent. It is the motivating conception in the long series of preliminary tests, in the mock killing of the candidate, in the baptismal rite, and in the sacred meal of bread and wine. Through the tests, moral as well as physical, courage and steadfastness were measured and developed. The pretended killing symbolized the end of the old impure life and implied the idea of a resurrection to a life of new and higher spirituality here and hereafter. Baptism, either by sprinkling or immersion, washed away the sins and impurities of the flesh. And finally the sacred commemorative meal, so well illustrated by the relief found at Konjica in Bosnia, brings the initiate into immediate communion with the divine Mithras. Data in regard to the details of many phases of Mithraic ritual are woefully

[2] Willoughby, *op. cit.*, 175.

inadequate, but some information is available from ancient authors, especially the Church Fathers. Among other curious things we are told that after baptism honey was put on the tongue of the initiate, apparently in the belief that it was a medium of spiritual growth. It is reported also that the initiates were branded on the forehead as a sign of adherence to the faith and even as a means of identification by the god himself. If we could accept Dieterich's [3] view that part of the contents of a magical papyrus found in Egypt belongs to a Mithraic liturgy, we should point to it as attesting with an unusual degree of clearness the importance of the doctrine of regeneration in Mithraism. But Dieterich has not established his case. It must, however, be added that while this document does not refer to Mithraism, it furnishes incontestable evidence of the prevalence of the idea of regeneration in the religious conceptions of the third and fourth centuries of our era. For in its text we find some of the most striking expressions of the idea of spiritual rebirth.

Other influences also were active in the pagan world in the propagation of the doctrine of re-

[3] *Eine Mithrasliturgie.*

generation. The Orphics taught the possibility of regeneration and final salvation through cycles of incarnation and purgatorial suffering. The doctrines of the Neopythagoreans followed the same lines. As further evidence of the prevalence of the idea of regeneration we may cite the Hermetic literature, for although the compilation of this Corpus may not have taken place till the end of the third century, some of the tractates are as early as the first century.[4] In these writings, especially in the dialogue between Hermes and his son Tat, regeneration has a notably prominent place.

Finally pagan philosophy was helping to build up the belief in regeneration. Neoplatonism, which had great influence in the first three centuries of the Christian era, constructed as it was on the basis of passages in Plato's dialogues which dealt with the aspiration of the soul toward the ultimate source of all that was good and beautiful, taught the possibility of purification from sin and the communion of the soul with God. And Stoicism, which in the age just before the end of the Republic and during the first centuries of the Christian era constituted the religion or at least was the chief

[4] Reitzenstein, *Poimandres,* 11 ff.

ethical control of many Romans of the cultured class, turned men's minds in the same direction. The ideas of freeing the soul from evil, of communing with the divine, and even of instantaneous regeneration appear in the writings of the Stoic philosophers. It was from Stoicism that Cicero drew the phrase " not emended but transfigured." [5]

The theories of regeneration mentioned above tell their own story, and it is hardly necessary to point to the similar doctrines that form an important part of Christian teaching. The purifying power of baptism, communion with God through sacred meals or other media, and the higher spiritual life that could be thus attained, redemption through a god who died and rose again, hell, purgatory, and heaven are all parts of the common stock of religious ideas that were current in the first centuries of the Christian Church. Large numbers of those who listened to the early preachers of Christianity were, from their knowledge of the mystery religions, wholly familiar with many of the doctrines of the new faith. Nor is it possible or even important to indicate from what particular source — Isiac, Mithraic, Orphic, or

[5] On whole subject see Willoughby, *op. cit.*, 221 ff., 269 ff.

other — the Christians drew this or that doctrine. Justin Martyr's remark on the imitation of Christian rites by the Mithraists has
already been quoted. Perhaps his statement in
regard to the matter was true so far as it went,
but there is every reason to believe that the imitation was not always on one side. In addition to the fundamental fact of the general
prevalence of the idea of regeneration and
of certain methods of consummating it there
doubtless was inter-action among the different
religions, and what had proved effective propaganda material for one cult was sometimes
adopted by another. For example the branding
of initiates of Mithras on the forehead may
perhaps be the source of the custom that prevailed among some Gnostic sects of branding
adherents on the right ear. And here too we
may see the ultimate origin of the present custom of making the sign of the cross over candi-
dates for baptism and confirmation.

XXX. CONCEPTIONS OF THE AFTER–LIFE

THE ROMANS of the early period had only the vaguest ideas about the condition and nature of souls after death. It is, however, clear that they conceived of them as living, and if not always active, at least capable of action. In their belief apparently, if burial rites were properly performed and the customary offerings at the tomb duly made, the spirits were likely to be quiescent. But if these ceremonies were neglected, they would become hostile. Whatever activity the Romans attributed to them they thought of as being manifested in the affairs of this world, especially in those of the families to which they belonged. The idea of a hell does not appear in early Roman religion.

But when Greek religious beliefs became current in Rome, the idea of an abode for the spirits of the dead — a place of torture for the damned and an elysium for the innocent — situated somewhere under the earth became more and more familiar. Nor can we say that ideas of this kind existed only among those whose culture included a knowledge of the literature and religion of the Greeks. To be sure it was chiefly through them that such beliefs spread, but that they did reach many of the less cultured classes seems beyond question. It is hardly likely that Lucretius would have written as he did about the horrors and absurdities of Hades unless there had been in his time a considerable volume of belief of this kind.

Greek influence in this field, however, was not confined to the spread of such ideas about the lower world as are found in Homer. Much more potent was the influence of the Eleusinian Mysteries and Orphic doctrines. The former made a profound impression upon Graeco-Roman society; and Orphism was established in southern Italy as early as the fifth century before Christ. It preceded Pythagoreanism in that region and many of its doctrines were adopted by the Pythagoreans. Both in the Eleusinian Mysteries and in Orphism the doctrine of hell involves not merely the idea of punishment for sins committed in this life but also purgatorial suffering through which one might ultimately attain purity and that eternity of happiness which is its reward.

Doubtless also the various Greek stories about descents to hell, such as those of Orpheus, who went down to rescue Eurydice, Dionysus who made the descent in search of Semele, Theseus and Pirithous who planned to carry off Persephone herself, and Castor and Pollux — all of which are frequently mentioned by the Latin poets — helped to disseminate the idea of a hell.

An important document for the study of the religious attitude of the time is the sixth book of Virgil's *Aeneid*. It is a link between the age of Augustus and the Christian era. This is especially true of that passage where the poet seems to give expression to his belief on the question of life and death. The lines are of notable significance. He speaks as though he were a seer in the highest sense of the word and were distilling the truth out of the confused mass of the religious thinking and philosophical speculation of the age. His period was one of transition in the history of religion. Prescott [1] has aptly said that " the sixth *Aeneid* is a bridge between paganism and Christianity." The old Roman religion had broken down. Thoughtful men had turned to philosophy. Some of Vir-

[1] Prescott, *The Development of Virgil's Art*, 427.

gil's lines in this part of the sixth book might serve as an outline of the belief of an advanced theist of our own day. For example these:

One Life through all the immense creation runs,
One Spirit is the moon's, the sea's, the sun's;
All forms in the air that fly, on the earth that creep,
And the unknown nameless monsters of the deep, —
Each breathing thing obeys one Mind's control,
And in all substance is a single Soul.
First to each seed a fiery force is given;
And every creature was begot in heaven;
Only their flight must hateful flesh delay
And gross limbs moribund and cumbering clay.
So from that hindering prison and night forlorn
Thy hopes and fears, thy joys and woes are born,
Who only seest, till death dispart thy gloom,
The true world glow through crannies of a tomb.[2]

He had struck a similar note in a passage in the *Georgics* (IV. 223 ff.):

Then since from God those lesser lives began,
And the eager spirits entered into man,
To God again the enfranchised soul must tend,
He is her home, her Author is her End;
No death is hers; when earthly eyes grow dim,
Starlike she soars and Godlike melts in Him.[3]

[2] Translation by Myers, *Essays-Classical*, 173.
[3] Translation by Myers, *ibid.*

There were other influences also. The cults of the Great Mother, Isis, and Mithras stressed, as a telling part of their propaganda, the certainty of a blessed immortality. According to the teaching of the Mithraists, more-over, the soul of the devotee, purified by the rites connected with the seven successive degrees of initiation, passed through the seven spheres that lie between the earth and the upper regions of the sky and found its final resting-place in a heaven among the fixed stars.[4]

The influence of these pagan cults, together with that of Jewish teaching — for the Jews also placed the souls of the dead beneath the earth — is manifest in Christian doctrines of eschatology. Probably the mystery religions, chiefly through the scenes of their initiation ceremonies, made the largest contribution to the building up of those ideas of the ultimate destiny of the soul which from the second or third century on through the Middle Ages dominated Christian teaching and have not entirely disappeared today. Indeed, in the doctrines of the

[4] There is a good discussion of the whole question of the attitude of the ancients toward the after-life in Clifford H. Moore's *Pagan Ideas of Immortality during the Early Roman Empire*.

less advanced forms of Christianity there are, with numerous and manifest modifications and changes, substantial remains of the old Homeric ideas of a hell for the wicked and a paradise for the blessed as well as of those beliefs in regard to the efficacy of purgatorial suffering which find their origin in the mystery religions. For the influence of the Mithraic conception of a heaven among the fixed stars the case is not so clear.

Nor is it unlikely that the story of the descent of Jesus into hell has been influenced by the stories of similar descents by pagan heroes referred to above.[5] Those [6] who on the ground of dissimilarities in the stories scout this theory as " unproved " and " in the highest degree improbable " do not make out a very strong case. Of course, there are differences in the stories; in each case — pagan or Christian — the setting is different. But none the less all the stories belong to the same class. The descent-idea was a part of the general fund of religious ideas in Graeco-Roman times.

[5] Clemen, *Religionsgesch. Erklärung d. N. T.;* Gardner, *Exploratio Evangelica,* 263–74.

[6] See Friedrich Loofs in *E. R. E.,* IV. 651.

XXXI. MATERIAL REMAINS

MANY material remains of the various cults practiced by the Romans may still be seen. These consist of pagan temples that have been converted into churches; of statues originally pagan that have been adapted to Christian usage; of statues, frescoes, or mosaics that while belonging to the Christian era show the influence of pagan art; and of certain other miscellaneous relics.

1. PAGAN TEMPLES USED AS CHRISTIAN CHURCHES

OF THE Roman temples taken over by the Church the most famous was the Pantheon, erected in the Campus Martius in 27 B.C. by Agrippa, minister of Augustus. Early in the seventh century it was dedicated by Pope Boniface IV as the church of S. Maria ad Martyres, and for more than thirteen centuries it has been used for Christian services. Another example which in spite of the doubt about the identification of the remains may be mentioned, is the temple of Augustus, built by Tiberius, part of which was converted before the sixth century into the church of S. Maria Antiqua. The latter was replaced in the ninth century by the church of S. Maria Nuova, on the site of which in turn the basilica of S. Maria Liberatrice was erected in the thirteenth century.[1] The temple of the deified emperor Antoninus and his wife Faustina in the Forum became in the seventh or eighth century the church of S. Lorenzo in Miranda. The Ionic temple in the Forum Boarium, possibly a sanctuary of Mater Matuta, was changed into the church of S. Maria Egiziaca in 872. The small round temple in the same neighborhood, which with some degree of plausibility has been identified as the temple of Portunus, was the church of S. Stephano Rotondo in the twelfth century, of S. Stephano delle Carrozze in the sixteenth, and later became the church S. Maria del Sole.

Nor was it in Rome only that pagan temples were used for Christian purposes. The so-called temple of the Sibyl at Tivoli was used as a church in the Middle Ages. At Cori in the Volscian hills part of the so-called temple of

[1] Platner and Ashby, *Topographical Dictionary of Ancient Rome,* 62 ff.

Hercules was incorporated with the church of
S. Pietro. At Nola a temple of Victory became
the church of the martyr Victoria. In the same
town a temple of Apollo was converted into a
church of Christ, and some of the attributes and
functions of the pagan deity were transferred
to his successor. On a promontory near Croton
on the east coast of Bruttium in southern Italy
once stood a temple of Hera, the religious cen-
ter for all the Greek colonies along that coast
and the objective of great pilgrimages, whither
each year a gorgeous procession passed, as in
Athens to the Parthenon. A temple of forty-
eight columns it was, set in a grove of pine-
trees. There was great treasure deposited there
also, which even Hannibal feared to touch.
When the Romans conquered this part of Italy,
they merely changed the name of the goddess
from Hera to Juno Lucina. Then in the fifth
century the Bishop of Croton made the temple
into a church and instead of Juno the Madonna
was worshipped there. But certain features of
the old cult remained. As before, processions
passed to the temple; as before, vows were
made and paid there; as before, women went
there in the crises of their lives. In pagan times
women used to lay down their ornaments before

the image of Hera or Juno; in a later age
Christian girls did the same when they renounced the world and entered a nunnery. The
temple stood till the sixteenth century. In
Sicily the Madonna has taken possession of
sanctuaries of Ceres and Venus, and the peasants have transferred to her the worship their
forbears once paid to her pagan predecessors.

In the instances cited above it was the actual
pagan building or at least part of it that was
used by the Church. There are many examples
also of pagan religious sites being used for
Christian worship. In some cases this was
nothing more than coincidence, in others there
was some degree of continuity of cult, while
doubtless in still others — and this is probably
true also of many of the buildings cited in the
preceding paragraphs — the Christians acted
deliberately, glorying in the displacement of
pagan by Christian rites and regarding it as a
sign manifest of the victory of the true religion.
The examples are numerous. About the middle
of the ninth century Pope Leo IV built the
church of S. Maria Nuova in the ruins of the
temple of Venus and Rome in the Forum. This
is now the church of S. Francesca Romana.
The church of SS. Cosma and Damiano is on

the site of the temple of the Penates as restored by Augustus.[2] The church of S. Maria
in Cosmedin is built partly on the remains of
an ancient temple, identified by some topog-
raphers as that of Hercules Pompeianus. Substantial ruins of a temple, the identification of
which is uncertain, lie beneath the church of
S. Niccolo ai Cesarini in the Campus Martius.
In the same region is the church of S. Stephano
del Cacco, which stands on the site of a temple
of Isis and Serapis. Its specific designation
(*Cacco*, " Baboon ") is derived from the figure
now in the Vatican gallery, which once formed
part of the decoration of the sacred avenue that
led to the double temple. At Terracina on the
coast of Latium the church of S. Caesareo
stands on the site of a temple of Caesar Augustus. The monastery founded on Monte Cassino
by Benedict in the sixth century was built on
the site of a temple of Apollo. Benedict is
said to have driven out the false god Apollo
with holy water and to have established St.
Martin there. Thus the bow-bearing Apollo
yielded to St. Martin, but the bow still remains
as an attribute of the Saint. One of the oldest
churches of the Madonna in Naples is built

[2] Platner and Ashby, *op. cit.,* 389.

on the ruins of a temple of Diana, and it may easily be that the prayers which matrons today address to the Madonna do not differ very much in content from those formerly made to Diana. In Naples a church of John the Baptist occupied the site of a temple of Antinous, the favorite of Hadrian, who was deified at the instance of the latter. The church of S. Restituta, which adjoins the cathedral in Naples, is said to be built on the site of a temple of Apollo, and the ancient columns in the nave are supposed to have originally belonged to that structure. There is a church of St. Paul in Pozzuoli on the site of a temple of Castor and Pollux where statues of Peter and Paul have replaced the statues of the Dioscuri. At Posilipo the church of the Madonna del Faro has been built on the site of a shrine of Venus Eupleia, and like its pagan prototype is much frequented by sea-farers. In Nola it was a temple of Jupiter that yielded its site to the basilica of St. Felix, wonder-worker and patron of the town. In Meta near Sorrento there is the church of a Madonna who performs marvels of healing similar to those which Minerva Medica formerly wrought on the same site. In Messina the church of St. Gregory occupies the site of a

temple of Jupiter. At Marsala a church of St.
John has been erected above the cave and magic
spring of an ancient Sibyl, and the place long
retained a reputation for oracular responses.
On the western promontory of Sicily there is a
famous statue of the Madonna on the site of
the ancient temple of Venus Erycina.

2. Statues, Reliefs, Frescoes and Mosaics

In a few cases ancient statues have been
adapted to Christian worship. The torso of
S. Helena in the church of S. Croce in Gerusa-
lemme, in Rome, probably once belonged to a
statue of Juno with a scepter in the right hand
and a vase in the left. A cross has been substituted for the scepter and a nail from the cross
for the vase. The figure of S. Sebastiano in
the church of S. Agnese in the piazza Navona
is an adaptation of an ancient statue. A statue
of Ariadne on the banks of a stream near Mon-
teleone in southern Italy is used today as a
representation of S. Venere. The tomb of the
poet Sannazaro in the church of S. Maria del
Parto in Naples has a bas-relief with figures of
Neptune, Pan, and nymphs, and on either side
statues of Apollo and Minerva. It was not till

the eighteenth century that the Apollo was inscribed with the name of David and the Minerva with that of Judith.[3]

But although the number of pagan statues that have been used in Christian worship is relatively small, there are numerous examples of the influence of Graeco-Roman art on Christian representations of divinity or saints. While there is no possibility that the well-known statue of St. Peter in his basilica in Rome is an adaptation of a statue of Jupiter nor any reason for believing that the keys have been substituted for a thunder-bolt, it doubtless does show the influence of pagan statues of seated divinities. To this same Graeco-Roman type of a seated divinity, if not to an ultimate prototype in Assyrian sculpture, may be traced also some of the Christian representations of God the Father as an old man seated on a throne. Moreover, the pagan multiple-headed divinities such as Hecate with three, Hermes with two, three, or four, and Janus with two heads survived in the Christian representations of the Trinity with three heads or three faces and even in those of Satan who is occasionally depicted with three faces.

[3] Lanciani, *Pagan and Christian Rome*, 25.

While the early type of Christ, without beard, is thought by some to show reminiscences of the Graeco-Roman Apollo, there is a much clearer case of pagan influence in the representation of Christ as the Good Shepherd with a lamb on his shoulders. Going back as it does to the statue of Hermes carrying a ram (the original of which seems to have been a priest bearing a victim to sacrifice), this figure, in its preservation of the essential elements of the original with a complete change of symbolism, constitutes an unusually good example of the relation of Christian to pagan art. In a number of paintings and reliefs found in the catacombs Orpheus is substituted for the Good Shepherd. In these he is playing on his lyre as he watches his flock. In other representations Orpheus, taming wild animals, symbolizes Christ instructing mankind.

The pagan Sibyls became an important element in Christian art. It was believed that the Sibyl of Tibur had prophesied to Augustus the coming of Christ, and the traditional explanation of the name of the church of S. Maria in Aracoeli, erected in the ninth century on the Capitoline hill, is that it occupies the site of the altar erected by Augustus after the revelation. This tradition finds expression in the companion paintings of Augustus and of the Sibyl on the walls on either side of the arch behind the high altar. Michelangelo incorporated the Sibyls in his paintings in the Sistine Chapel; Raphael painted them in the church of S. Maria della Pace, where they are represented as recording the revelations imparted to them by angels; Pinturicchio depicted them in the Borgia apartments. They appear also in the Casa Santa at Loreto and in the pavement of the cathedral at Siena.

There are many other adoptions or adaptions. Psyche, who already symbolized the soul in pagan art, was used in the same way by the Church. Christian sarcophagi of the fourth and fifth centuries reproduce in their bas-reliefs pagan scenes of genii busy with the vintage, the vine here being the true vine. The same decorative motive is employed in the blue mosaics of the fourth century in the vaulting of the ambulatory of S. Costanza. The peacock which belonged to the Hera-Juno cult became an emblem of the resurrection. In pagan art also originated that extensive use of the nimbus found on Christian monuments. Among the pagans it was used in the representation of sun-gods; in some cases rays were made to emanate from the head; in others the nimbus had the form of a circular disk behind the head. The Christian development showed variety of form and greatly increased frequency of use. Sometimes the nimbus was circular, sometimes triangular; in other examples, it was square, in still others (especially in the case of divine persons) it was cruciform. It was used for the heads of the persons of the Trinity, the Madonna, angels, and saints. The immediate source of the Christian nimbus may have been the representation of the sun-god, with rays shooting from his head, found on monuments of Mithras. However this may be, Mithraic art is certainly responsible for other elements on Christian monuments: for example, the images of the sun and moon, ocean, earth and sky, the signs of the Zodiac, the winds, and the seasons.

Pagan and Christian motives were often used together. In the church of S. Andrea, constructed by Pope Simplicius in the fifth century out of the basilica of Bassus on the Esquiline hill in Rome, mosaics of Christ and his apostles were combined with others of Diana, Hylas, and the Great Mother. These survived till the sixteenth century. Among the bas-reliefs that adorned the side-walls of the church of S. Martina, built in the ruins of the Secretarium Senatus, an annex to the Senate House, there was one which represented the emperor Marcus Aurelius sacrificing to Jupiter. This is now in the Palazzo dei Conservatori. The doors of St. Peter's show a strange contrast of Christian and pagan subjects, for while the main panels are decorated with Christian motives, the borders are adorned with such scenes as Phrixus and Helle on the ram, Europa on the bull, Ganymede and the eagle, and Leda with the swan.

That the Christians should have used so freely the plastic and pictorial inheritance that had come down to them from Roman times is not surprising. Their practice presents nothing novel in the history of religion. The adherents of other faiths have done the same. The followers of Buddha have been equally quick to adapt the images of the cults which their faith has superseded. Nor has Christian practice confined itself to the use of Greek or Roman images or motives. Leroy-Beaulieu [4] tells us that there is an old Buriat idol in a monastery on Lake Baikal that has been trans-

[4] *La religion dans l'empire des Tsars*, 113.

formed into a statue of St. Nicholas and is worshipped with equal zeal by Christian and non-
Christian devotees.

3. Altars and Street Shrines

Pagan altars sometimes found a place in Christian churches. Till the eighteenth century an
ancient altar supported the high altar in the
church of S. Teodoro in Rome. Another, in
the church of S. Michele in Gorgo, was adorned
with bas-reliefs of the Great Mother and Attis.
The altar now in the Capitoline museum, which
some devotee of Isis dedicated to the goddess in
gratitude for her protection during a journey,
long stood in the church of Aracoeli, and in the
same place there was another to the goddess
Annona.

4. Ancient Standards of Weight

The round black stones that may be seen in
some churches in Rome constitute a curious
survival from pagan times. These stones,
sometimes explained in connection with the
martyrdom of saints, are nothing more than
standard weights which the Romans used to
keep in their temples. When churches superseded the temples, the weights were transferred,

and doubtless at first were used for their proper purpose. In the course of time, however, and with change of customs their significance was lost sight of. The best set is that in the church of S. Maria in Trastevere.

5. The Inscription on the Arch of Constantine

Even the Arch of Constantine in Rome built in A.D. 316 to commemorate Constantine's victory over Maxentius in 312 shows a blending of pagan and Christian elements. For while on the most plausible interpretation the words of the inscription, *instinctu divinitatis* (" through the inspiration of God "), ascribe the victory over the tyrant to the aid of the God of the Christians, other parts of the arch are adorned with reliefs taken partly from a building of the period of Hadrian and partly from some monument of the Antonine age and representing scenes of pagan sacrifice. To be sure, the reference to Christianity lacks definiteness, but probably this was intentional. It was a compromise between the pagan and Christian parties in the state. The pagans could interpret it as a recognition of any god in their pantheon; to the Christians it meant only Christ. Physically this arch stands at the beginning of the road that runs between the Palatine and the Caelian, but spiritually it marks the parting of the ways in the religious history of Rome.

BIBLIOGRAPHY

BIBLIOGRAPHY

1. GENERAL

AUST, A., *De aedibus sacris populi Romani.* Marburg, 1889.

BOUCHÉ-LECLERCQ, A., *Histoire de la divination dans l'antiquité.* Paris, 1879.

BOULAGE, T. P., *Les mystères d'Isis et d'Osiris.* Paris, 1912.

BUREL, J., *Isis et Isiaques sous l'empire romain.* Paris, 1911.

CARTER, J. B., *The Religious Life of Ancient Rome.* Boston and New York, 1911.

CUMONT, F., *Textes et monuments figurés relatifs aux mystères de Mithra.* Avec une introduction critique. Bruxelles, t. 1. Introduction, 1899; t. 2. Textes et monuments, 1896.

CUMONT, F., *Les mystères de Mithra.* Bruxelles, 1913.[3] English translation of earlier edition by T. J. McCormack, Chicago, 1903.

CUMONT, F., *Les Religions orientales dans le paganisme romain.* Paris, 1930.[3] English translation of earlier edition by Grant Showerman under the title *Oriental Religions in Roman Paganism.* Chicago, 1911.

CUMONT, F., *Astrology and Religion among Greeks and Romans.* New York, 1912.

CUMONT, F., *After Life in Roman Paganism.* Lectures delivered at Yale University on the Silliman Foundation. New Haven, 1922.

FOWLER, W. WARDE, *The Roman Festivals of the Period of the Republic.* An Introduction to the Study of the Religion of the Romans. London, 1899.

FOWLER, W. WARDE, *The Religious Experience of the Roman People.* From the Earliest Times to the Age of Augustus. The Gifford Lectures for 1909–10. London, 1911.

FOWLER, W. WARDE, *Roman Ideas of Deity in the Last Century before the Christian Era.* London, 1914.

[253]

GASQUET, A. L., *Le culte et les mystères de Mithra.* Paris, 1899.

GRAILLOT, H., *Le culte de Cybèle, Mère des Dieux, à Rome et dans l'empire romain.* Paris, 1912.

GRANGER, F., *The Worship of the Romans.* London, 1895.

HALLIDAY, W. R., *Lectures on the History of Roman Religion.* Liverpool and London, 1922.

HASTINGS, J., *Encyclopaedia of Religion and Ethics.* New York and Edinburgh, 1922.

HEPDING, H., *Attis, seine Mythen und sein Kult.* Giessen, 1903.

HERBERMAN, C. G., and others, *The Catholic Encyclopedia.* New York, 1907–22.

DE JONG, K. H. E., *Das antike Mysterienwesen.* Leyden, 1919.[2]

LAFAYE, G., *Histoire du culte des divinités d'Alexandrie.* Paris, 1884.

LANCIANI, R., *Ancient Rome in the Light of Recent Discoveries.* Boston and New York, 1888.

LANCIANI, R., *The Ruins and Excavations of Ancient Rome.* Boston and New York, 1897.

MACCHIORO, V., *Roma Capta.* Saggio intorno alla religione romana. Messina, 1928.

DE-MARCHI, A., *Il culto privato di Roma antica.* 2 vols. Milano, 1896–1903.

MARQUARDT, J., *Das Sacralwesen* (Römische Staatsverwaltung, dritter Band, besorgt von Georg Wissowa. Leipzig, 1885).

MAU, A., *Pompeii: Its Life and Art.* Translated into English by F. W. Kelsey. New York, 1907.

MOORE, C. H., *Pagan Ideas of Immortality during the Early Roman Empire.* Cambridge (Mass.), 1918.

MOORE, G. F., *History of Religions.* 2 vols. New York, 1920.[2]

PAULY-WISSOWA-KROLL, *Real-Encyclopädie der classischen Altertumswissenschaft.* Stuttgart, 1894.

PEASE, A. S., *M. Tulli Ciceronis de divinatione libri.* With commentary. In University of Illinois Studies in Language and Literature, Vol. VI, nos. 2 and 3, Urbana, Illinois, 1920, and Vol. VIII, nos. 2 and 3.

BIBLIOGRAPHY

PLATNER, S. B., *The Topography and Monuments of Ancient Rome*. Boston, 1911.[2]

PLATNER, S. B., *A Topographical Dictionary of Ancient Rome*. Completed and revised by Thomas Ashby. London, 1929.

PRELLER, L., *Römische Mythologie*. 3. Auflage von H. Jordan. 2 vols. Berlin, 1881–83.

PRESCOTT, HENRY W., *The Development of Virgil's Art*. Chicago, 1927.

ROSCHER, W. H., *Ausführliches Lexikon der griechischen und römischen Mythologie*. Leipzig, 1884.

ROSE, H. J., *Primitive Culture in Italy*. London and New York, 1926.

SAMTER, E., *Familienfeste der Griechen und Römer*. Berlin, 1901.

SHOWERMAN, GRANT, *The Great Mother of the Gods*. Madison, Wisconsin, 1901.

STRONG, MRS. ARTHUR, *Roman Sculpture from Augustus to Constantine*. London and New York, 1907.

STRONG, MRS. ARTHUR, *Apotheosis and After Life*. New York, 1915.

TOUTAIN, J., *Les cultes païens dans l'empire romain*. 3 vols. Paris, 1907–1917.

WISSOWA, G., *Religion und Kultus der Römer*. München, 1912.[2] In Iwan von Müller, Handbuch der Klassischen Altertumswissenschaft, V. 4.

2. OF SPECIAL INTEREST FOR THE STUDY OF SURVIVALS

ANGUS, S., *The Environment of Early Christianity*. New York, 1915.

ANGUS, S., *The Mystery-Religions and Christianity*. A Study in the Religious Background of Early Christianity. London, 1925.

ANGUS, S., *The Religious Quests of the Graeco-Roman World*. A Study in the Historical Background of Early Christianity. New York, 1929.

BAILEY, CYRIL, *The Legacy of Rome* (chap. on Religion and Philosophy, pp. 237–264). Oxford, 1924.

BRAND, J., *Observations on the Popular Antiquities of Great Britain*. Revised by Sir Henry Ellis. Bohn's Antiquarian Library. 3 vols. London, 1890.

BUDGE, E. H. T. W., *Osiris and the Egyptian Resurrection*. London, 1911.

CASE, S. J., *The Evolution of Early Christianity*. Chicago, 1914.

CASE, S. J., *The Social Origins of Christianity*. Chicago, 1923.

DIETERICH, A., *Eine Mithrasliturgie*. Leipzig, 1910.

DUCHESNE, L. M. O., *Early History of the Christian Church, from its Foundation to the End of the Fifth Century*. Rendered into English from the fourth edition. London, 1909–24.

DUCHESNE, L. M. O., *Christian Worship: Its Origin and Evolution*. A Study of the Latin Liturgy up to the time of Charlemagne. Translated by M. L. McClure. London, 1912.

FRAZER, J. G., *The Golden Bough*. A Study in Magic and Religion. London, 1911–1922.[3]

FRAZER, J. G., *The Fasti of Ovid*. Edited with a translation and commentary. 5 vols. London, 1929.

GARDNER, P., *Exploratio Evangelica; A Brief Examination of the Basis and Origin of Christian Belief*. New York, 1899.

GARDNER, P., *The Growth of Christianity*. London, 1907.

GLASSÉ, J., *The Mysteries and Christianity*. Edinburgh, 1921.

GLOVER, T. R., *The Conflict of Religions in the Early Roman Empire*. London, 1909.[2]

GLOVER, T. R., *Progress in Religion to the Christian Era*. London, 1922.

HALLIDAY, W. R., *The Pagan Background of Early Christianity*. Liverpool and London, 1925.

HAMILTON, M., *Incubation or the Cure of Disease in Pagan Temples and Christian Churches*. London, 1906.

HYDE, W. W., *Greek Religion and Its Survivals*. In series Our Debt to Greece and Rome. New York, 1923.

KENNEDY, H. A. A., *St. Paul and the Mystery Religions*. New York, 1913.

BIBLIOGRAPHY

LANCIANI, R., *Pagan and Christian Rome*. Boston and New York, 1892.

LEGGE, F., *Forerunners and Rivals of Christianity*. 2 vols. Cambridge, 1915.

LOISY, A. F., *Les mystères païens et le mystère chrétien*. Paris, 1921.[2]

McDANIEL, W. B., *Roman Private Life and Its Survivals*. In series Our Debt to Greece and Rome. New York, 1927.

MACCHIORO, V. D., *From Orpheus to Paul*. A History of Orphism. New York, 1930.

MANNHARDT, W., *Antike Wald- und Feld-kulte aus nordeuropäischer Ueberlieferung erläutert*. Berlin, 1904–5.[2]

MOORE, C. H., *Ancient Beliefs in the Immortality of the Soul*. In series Our Debt to Greece and Rome. New York, 1931.

PASCAL, C., *Feste e poesie antiche*. Milano, 1926.

PETRIE, W. M. FLINDERS, *Personal Religion in Egypt before Christianity*. New York, 1909.

REINACH, S., *Cults, Myths and Religions*. English translation by Elizabeth Frost. London, 1912.

REITZENSTEIN, R., *Die hellenistischen Mysterien-religionen*. Leipzig, 1927.[3]

ROSTOVTZEFF, M., *Mystic Italy*. New York, 1928.

SAMTER, E., *Geburt, Hochzeit und Tod*. Leipzig und Berlin, 1911.

TREDE, TH., *Das Heidentum in der römischen Kirche*. Gotha, 1889–91.

TREDE, TH., *Wunderglaube im Heidentum und in der alten Kirche*. Gotha, 1901.

TYLOR, E. B., *Primitive Culture*. 2 vols. New York, 1877.[2]

USENER, H., *Das Weihnachtsfest*. Bonn, 1889. In Religionsgeschichtliche Untersuchungen, Erster Theil.

WHITEHEAD, P. B., " The Church of SS. Cosma e Damiano," in *American Journal of Archaeology*, XXXI. 1–18 (1927).

WILLOUGHBY, H. R., *Pagan Regeneration*. Chicago, 1929.

Our Debt to Greece and Rome

AUTHORS AND TITLES

AUTHORS AND TITLES

AUTHORS AND TITLES

AESCHYLUS AND SOPHOCLES. *J. T. Sheppard.*

GREEK RELIGION. *Walter Woodburn Hyde.*

SURVIVALS OF ROMAN RELIGION. *Gordon J. Laing.*

MYTHOLOGY. *Jane Ellen Harrison.*

ANCIENT BELIEFS IN THE IMMORTALITY OF THE SOUL. *Clifford H. Moore.*

STAGE ANTIQUITIES. *James Turney Allen.*

PLAUTUS AND TERENCE. *Gilbert Norwood.*

ROMAN POLITICS. *Frank Frost Abbott.*

PSYCHOLOGY, ANCIENT AND MODERN. *G. S. Brett.*

ANCIENT AND MODERN ROME. *Rodolfo Lanciani.*

WARFARE BY LAND AND SEA. *Eugene S. McCartney.*

THE GREEK FATHERS. *James Marshall Campbell.*

GREEK BIOLOGY AND MEDICINE. *Henry Osborn Taylor.*

MATHEMATICS. *David Eugene Smith.*

LOVE OF NATURE AMONG THE GREEKS AND ROMANS. *H. R. Fairclough.*

ANCIENT WRITING AND ITS INFLUENCE. *B. L. Ullman.*

GREEK ART. *Arthur Fairbanks.*

ARCHITECTURE. *Alfred M. Brooks.*

ENGINEERING. *Alexander P. Gest.*

MODERN TRAITS IN OLD GREEK LIFE. *Charles Burton Gulick.*

ROMAN PRIVATE LIFE. *Walton Brooks McDaniel.*

GREEK AND ROMAN FOLKLORE. *William Reginald Halliday.*

ANCIENT EDUCATION. *J. F. Dobson.*